J.D. Spencer is a qualified international healer and counsellor, a trained yoga and meditation teacher, and food allergy specialist. She ran The Allergy and Natural Healing Centre in Somerset, Southern England, for 15 years. Whilst living in Spain, she had several healing clinics in Andalucía, along the coast, and was interviewed many times on television and radio. She sees past lives, clears negative energies from dwellings and helps remaining spirits to pass over. She also runs spiritual development groups.

Dedication

To my wonderful husband, John, and my children, Rachael, Chloe and Daniel.

J.D. Spencer

DIVINE COMMUNICATION

AUSTIN MACAULEY PUBLISHERS™

LONDON • CAMBRIDGE • NEW YORK • SHARJAH

A CIP catalogue record for this title is available from the British Library.

ISBN 9781788484053 (Paperback)
ISBN 9781788484060 (Hardback)
ISBN 9781788484077 (E-Book)

www.austinmacauley.com

First Published (2018)
Austin Macauley Publishers Ltd™
25 Canada Square
Canary Wharf
London
E14 5LQ

Acknowledgements

I am very grateful to all the staff at Austin Macauley for bringing this book into publication and for all their care and attention.

The Soul Lives On

Hilary had had an awful childhood; her mother drank, was very moody, often flew into rages and threatened her with a knife. She used to run away to a nearby farm and hide all day. As an only child, she was very lonely and unhappy. When she was 18, her mother committed suicide. Her father then wanted them to both commit suicide together, and this demand went on for many years.

He tried to commit suicide on the motorway. She was in her forties when she first came to me, severely depressed. As she entered the room, I felt a huge cloud of despair and negativity around her. I began working with her, giving her healing to uplift her spirits and clear the depression.

During various consultations, the story of her childhood emerged, and I was able to see her mother and father in the spirit world. They were not together, as her mother was in a darker place. There was a great deal of anger and resentment between them all. I began to pray for both her parents, and with help from spirit, we sent them love and healing. Hilary began to feel much better, and gradually over time, there was an improvement to both her parents. Eventually, her mother and father were united together in the spirit world.

My client wanted to talk to them and ask them many questions. We began sessions of communication between them, and in cases such as this, I call on the highest source of light and love for help, which, in this case, was Jesus. I have recounted details of some of the sessions with this client later on in the book.

The death of my own mother had overwhelmingly affected me and changed my life. Until something touches our soul in this way, we tend to just live our lives, taking things for granted and not thinking too much about other worlds. Although we know that we will all die at some stage, it is not until we are touched profoundly that we start to question life and all of its meaning.

Some months after my mother died, I was sat in a tiny waiting room with a few other people, waiting my turn to see a medium. I didn't believe in these things, wasn't sure what I was doing there, why had I come, and wondered if it was too late and was contemplating getting up and running out. A moment later, a door opened, and a tiny elderly lady with a pile of curly hair called me in to an even smaller room, just enough room for two chairs and a little table.

As I entered the room, and before I had even sat down, she was waving her arms and telling me that she could feel death, that my mother was there, she had not died long ago, that I was broken-hearted and so was my father. She told me that she longed to wrap my father in a big loving blanket and hold him in her arms. I was utterly overwhelmed. If I had been able to speak, and I was too stunned to do so, I wouldn't have got a word in anyway, as she didn't stop talking, so quickly I could hardly take it all in.

She continued at a great pace to give me messages from my mother: how much she missed my two children, how she was perfectly safe and happy and at peace and I needn't have been so upset. The lady then told me that my two children and my husband were nearby somewhere and that they had come with me. She told me the colour of my children's hair, one blond, one auburn.

She then told me, something which I could scarcely take in, that I was a healer, that I could take her practice over the next day but she wouldn't allow me to, her children were ready to do so. She went on to tell me of a healing federation I needed to join, but her words were bouncing off my brain. That visit had been my first experience of mediums, my first glimpse into the possibility that my mother wasn't really dead, after all, but living somewhere else, and it had a massive impact on my life. It was six months since my mother had died, and I was half out of my mind with grief. When we got back home, we packed up and drove up to Essex to see my father and then brought him back to stay with us.

The possibility to me, at that time, that the soul lived on somewhere else was the single most profoundly comforting information I could have received. The death of somebody you love is so utterly painful, so utterly devastating that it can almost destroy you, it is something so hard to grasp that this person you loved and held in your arms will never be there again for you to hold, love and enjoy. You think you will never recover, the pain is so immense and all consuming.

I had been brought up as a Christian, baptised and confirmed, but found the church's teachings about life after death very vague on these matters. My local vicar tried to comfort me, he was a dear friend of mine, and he did his best.

Even so, despite what she had told me, it was all beyond my comprehension. Although I didn't understand how my mother could be somewhere else and be sending me messages, I had to admit that the medium had told me things it was impossible for her to know. I had not made an appointment, she didn't know my name and could not possibly have seen us park 100 yards away when she had a waiting room full of people she was attending to. As for telling me I was a healer, I knew nothing about healing and I certainly knew of no federation in London. As I didn't have a clue how to find out, I decided to just wait and see what happened next.

That was many years ago, and I have been a healer now for over 37 years, giving healing to both people and animals. During that time, I trained and qualified with the National Federation of Spiritual Healers; I trained as a yoga teacher with the British Wheel of Yoga and learned Transcendental Meditation, later becoming a Siddha, which involves advanced meditation techniques, including levitation.

I further studied radiesthesia and techniques for detecting food allergies, including vitamin and mineral deficiencies, treating hundreds of people from all over the world. I began this service at a time when most people didn't believe or understand allergies and very little was known about this subject. I established The Allergy and Natural Healing Centre in Somerset, which ran successfully for 15 years, then later opened several healing centres in Southern Spain, where I lived for many years. The allergy tests have helped to cure hundreds of people, and it is quite astonishing to see the vast number of

11

different ailments which can be caused by the foods one consumes. The Which Magazine tested me, unbeknown to me, sending me dozens of allergy tests and informed me just before they published their findings. This brought me a great deal more work.

In addition, I was teaching several weekly yoga classes, which continued for 20 years in England and Spain. As I opened up spiritually, I began to see past lives around my patients during healings and this developed into a separate therapy, healing on a much more profound level. A further aspect of my work involves clearing and healing clients' homes and cleaning up negativity embedded there. In the spiritual and psychic development groups I run, we are helping souls who have passed over and need help to progress.

For some years now, angels, Archangels, Ascended Masters and highly evolved spiritual beings have been working with me both on a personal level and with my clients. There is so much to learn, and our spiritual sight opens up to other realms when we are ready and able to deal with it.

So many of us involved in spiritual development have deep longings to be more psychic and more able to see other levels of existence, but we cannot force it, and we have to be patient and wait, living a spiritual life in the meantime.

During a major crisis in my life many years later, when I was meditating very seriously, my Kundalini energy began to unleash and has resulted in extensive experiences and studies on this subject. I have written about some of this later in the book.

Healing and Yoga Begin

During the two years after my visit to that dear lady in Somerset, I was prompted by other people to begin healing. I went to see two astrologers who both told me I was a healer, but the last encounter was really the catalyst which got me going. I was staying in the south of France with two of my children, Danny who was nine and Rachael who was seven. My third child Chloe was still a baby and had stayed at home with her father. We were on a campsite by the beach and in the evenings, there were various activities laid on at a clubhouse. This particular evening, there were about 100 people in the room and two eccentric French magicians, a man and a lady, were entertaining us with tricks. All of a sudden, the gentleman looked across the room at me and stopped. "You," he said, "I want to come to you, I must tell you that you have great power; you need to use it but please be careful."

He then turned away and they continued with the next trick. At that moment, I jumped up, grabbed both children and fled back to our tent. We went to bed and I didn't sleep a wink the entire night. I just lay there in a state of fear and shock wondering what on earth he meant, and what on earth was I supposed to do about it. I realised that it was time to do something, I couldn't go on doing nothing, I had received so many messages now.

I was now faced with trying to work out what to do next. By this time, I had started my training to be a yoga teacher. During the few months after my mother had died, I kept becoming ill with what the doctors thought was kidney infection and they were putting me on antibiotics every few weeks, but to no avail. I got such a fright thinking my kidneys were on their way out, I bought a book on yoga and began immediately to do the exercises to stimulate the kidneys. I spent most of the first day doing yoga and by the following morning, all my symptoms had disappeared. I then knew I had discovered something quite magical. In fact, a new doctor told me she thought there had been nothing wrong with my kidneys and it was all my nerves gone to pieces after the death of my mother. Either way, yoga had cured me, and within 24 hours. It is a powerful practice which heals and strengthens the body and calms the mind, it further develops the soul.

This began my fascination with yoga and I practised it daily from then onwards becoming very proficient. A friend of mine convinced me to join a class which I did reluctantly, I thought I was already perfectly able to do any posture, but the class was run by a delightful and powerful man who taught me a great deal. Shortly afterwards, he, another yoga teacher in the class, and I joined a yoga teacher training course together to enlarge our understanding, which lasted two and a half years.

It was at a yoga day which we attended, being run by two elderly Indian gentlemen, that the idea came to me that they would probably be able to help me with some information about healing. After the day's session, I approached them and told them about the messages I had received and asked them how I was supposed to begin healing. They advised me to lay my hands on someone and pray. They said it was that simple. I promised them I would try.

Again, it was forgotten for several months until one day I noticed that my darling cat, Mafie, had a lump which was most alarming as we had recently lost our boxer dog Samantha to cancer, she had been almost 13. I was very upset and thought I must take the cat to the vet and the whole process of operations would begin again. After two weeks, the lump had grown and was about the size of a plum. Suddenly I remembered all the messages and thought; *here we go, let's try to heal her.* I sat her on my lap, put my hands on her and prayed. I said, "Dear God, please heal my cat Mafie." I didn't know what else to say. I had no idea what I was doing. Within 10 minutes, the lump had shrunk to half its size. The next day, I did the same thing and in another 10 minutes, the lump disappeared completely. She was 11 at that time and lived until she was 18 years old. Needless to say, I was utterly amazed and spent the next few days pacing the floor and pacing the garden trying to get my head round it in a complete state of wonder and bewilderment.

That was the beginning of my work as a healer. I found it very unnerving at first and practised on friends, family and neighbours to begin with. My second attempt was with a friend of ours who lived in France. He complained of tennis elbow and constant pain. I gave him a healing, he returned to France that day and I heard nothing from him. Speaking to him on the telephone about six months later, I casually asked him how his elbow was and he told me he had never had any pain since I gave him a healing. All that time I had been thinking it hadn't worked. He just assumed that I knew he was cured.

Absent healing was working too. My sister-in-law discovered a lump in her throat and she was told it would have to be operated on two weeks later. She rang me and asked if I could send her absent healing as she lived in Essex. Twice a day for two weeks, I prayed and sent her healing. My brother took her to the hospital on the day of the operation and left her. The doctors examined her just before taking her down to the operating theatre and were utterly amazed to find that the lump had disappeared. Several doctors were called to examine her and they couldn't understand how it could have disappeared. They told her to go home. She caught a taxi and walked into the kitchen to find my astonished brother washing up. He told me later that she had spent a couple of hours just gazing out of the window as though in a trance, so overjoyed that an operation had been averted.

Childhood Experiences

I am often asked if my healing gift was apparent as a child. From a very young age, I did get very involved in helping animals, and there were many occasions when I arrived home with abandoned cats and dogs. On my way to infant school, I heard mewing from a dustbin and found half a dozen kittens placed in the rubbish. I carted them all home but my mother used to make me take them all to the local police station and I would vigorously question the policeman in charge exactly how he would care for them and what would happen to them, being all of about eight years old. I brought several stray dogs home and again I had to take them to the police station, we just didn't have the room for so many abandoned animals and our own dog would go completely crazy. I would get some food for them, feed them in the street and then tie them with some string and set off to the police station.

If I saw what I thought was any unkindness to horses, I would go berserk. Horses and carts were quite abundant in my childhood, and I recall crawling into the back of a covered cart and getting out a pile of blankets and covering the horse stood in torrential rain. When I thought one man was whipping his horse to go faster, I ran after the cart, laden with logs, climbed on the back and hurled logs of wood at the man – not at all sensible I must admit. Our local milkman came every day, and I always had bread and carrots waiting for the horse, he would climb up the pavement and pull the cart up behind him, straining to get my attention over the fence.

I had two big tanks of fish and I guess I was about seven when I did what must have been my first healing. One of my fish had flipped over on his side and it looked decidedly poorly, floating on the top of the water. It was still breathing so I sat up the whole night holding him upright until I felt he was better and could swim normally. As for any psychic background, the only thing I remember in that regard is my mother, father and grandmother sitting around the table and trying to teach me how to read tea leaves.

Clairvoyance Opening Up

As I worked with healing, my clairvoyant sight began to open. Pamela came complaining of a bladder problem which she had had for about 20 years, and after endless treatments, it still wasn't cured. As soon as I laid my hands on her, I felt a child had been killed. I was very disconcerted and alarmed wondering what had happened. I stayed calm and continued with the healing and after some minutes, I asked Pamela if a child had died in her life. She then burst into tears and said that when she was about 19, she had had an abortion and had bitterly regretted it ever since. She was racked with guilt and worry about the event, and had never come to terms with her decision and her loss. As we worked with these emotions and she slowly was able to forgive herself, her condition began to improve. This particular case took about six months to heal.

I began to see inside bodies and many cases have astonished me. Sandra was a beautiful young woman of mixed race who appeared outwardly to be in good health. She was, however, feeling very unwell and as I laid my hands on her shoulders, I saw inside her body, and her liver was decidedly abnormal. Half of it seemed to be perfectly normal and the other half looked wasted and moth eaten. Unsure why this would be, I gingerly asked her if she drank alcohol. "Oh yes," she said, quite cheerfully, "I drink a bottle of champagne every day starting with a big glass for breakfast, and I also drink wine and other spirits." I told her what it was doing to her liver and she was very shocked. She had a few healings with me until she felt considerably better and she promised to give up alcohol. The liver will recover if it is not too far-gone if alcohol is avoided and lots of water is drunk. I have seen this happening with my psychic vision.

Healing is not about religion, any person of any faith can receive healing, but some people do fret about it thinking it may interfere with their religious beliefs. A young lady rang me saying she desperately needed healing but her husband would not allow her to visit me alone, he insisted on coming with her and bringing their child. They both had different religious beliefs; he asked a great many questions before we began and insisted on staying in the same room with us. He sat very close to me, barely a yard away and didn't take his eyes off me for a second, staring very intently at me the whole time. This was hardly ideal for me and certainly was not a relaxing healing for the young lady; although she said she felt considerably better afterwards. Unfortunately, she rang me up afterwards and said although she had enjoyed it, felt much better and would love to come again, her husband had forbidden her.

A further aspect of my work involves clearing and healing people's homes, cleaning up negativity and also sending on spirits who have been unable to pass over for various reasons. People's homes accumulate a great deal of stress over the years and the older the house, the more stress and negativity it may hold. Negativity can be stuck there for centuries and arguments, fights, worries and illnesses can leave behind very low energies which can then adversely affect the inhabitants. Homes need healing with white light and all lower energies sent down into the earth to be transmuted back into white light. During cleansings, I have seen masses of grey matter pouring from the walls. A home can feel so much lighter after such a cleansing.

In addition to spiritual healing, I was seeing a lot of clients for allergy testing and vitamin and mineral deficiency testing, and these tests were helping to cure people of a huge variety of different ailments. I can sometimes look at someone and see exactly which food is making them ill. By now, I was also running two and sometimes three yoga classes a week, which ran for 10 years in England and a further eight years in Spain. Yoga is a powerful practice for healing and strengthening the body and mind and awakening spirituality, and many participants in my yoga classes were being healed of an assortment of ailments.

I am often so surprised that it hardly ever occurs to the average person to even make any attempt to heal themselves. I have noticed such closed minds to anything outside a doctor's surgery. A simple example of this was one afternoon, whilst I was waiting for my children to come out of school. I was talking to a neighbour and the mother of one of my son's best friends, and she was telling me that she had had a bad cough for some weeks and had taken a lot of medicine the doctor had prescribed for her and nothing had helped her. I suggested that she took several cups of thyme tea a day at which she laughed heartily and said, "You have to be kidding, that sounds ridiculous." She had thyme plants in her garden and I urged her to try the tea. About three days later, I saw her and she told me that her cough had gone and she was simply amazed. She was also very embarrassed.

As a healer, I have been laughed at and mocked so many times in my life. I have been stared at with pity and condescension. Occasionally, someone gets angry with me and asks why on earth can I heal and they can't. One has to learn to ignore it and rise above it, after all, ignorance is prevalent everywhere. Now at least healers are not being tortured with terrible instruments, burned alive and drowned by the church as healers were during the Inquisition.

We owned a house in Spain for 20 years and lived there for eight years; the whole story with endless dramas is described in my book *Calamares and Corruption*. I had hundreds of patients in Spain after I gave a television interview and had several clinics there. I recall a time when each week for several weeks, I had a local policeman come to me for healing and I was considerably uneasy about his intentions – I was very nervous that he may be investigating me. However, he had had a nervous breakdown, wasn't able to work anymore and was grateful to feel much better receiving healing, for which he paid me with a loaf of delicious homemade bread he had made for me each time.

In Somerset, we had a thriving business on our premises, my husband had a garage involving body work and repairs, buying and selling cars, and one of his customers was our local doctor who invited us to a party he was holding. There were 12 doctors at the party and every single one of them had a go at me, knowing I was a healer, asking questions and generally mocking healing and all forms of alternative medicine. Three or four of them got me in a corner and even guffawed loudly together at the very notion of aromatherapy, food allergies and reflexology. I am always amazed at the arrogance of doctors who think that only toxic medicines will cure the body.

There is, however, considerable improvement nowadays in this area with younger doctors open to alternative medicine, they have had no option but to look at it; it is so prevalent. A young friend of ours training to be a doctor had to look at alternative medicine for his degree.

My Son in Trouble

My husband received a telephone call from the hospital to say our son, Daniel, had had a motorbike accident and would I come straight in. I had just picked up a small excited child from her home to come and play for the first time with our youngest daughter Chloe, she had been in our house all of ten minutes at this point. Then a few minutes later, Danny rang me and said he was in a great deal of pain and the doctors were going to operate and would I go in straight away. I had to bundle our young visitor hastily into the car and take her home again and we sped off to the hospital.

When we arrived, Dan was surrounded by five or six doctors who were considering operating and I burst in and said would you all please leave, I am his mother, I am a healer and I shall heal him. Amazingly, they all turned away and left the room. Dan was in a great deal of abdominal pain, from where the handlebars of his motor bike had banged into his stomach at the accident. He also had a broken hip. A motorist had pulled out of a side road and smashed into him. Someone I know had seen him lying in the road, not knowing who he was, and had thought him dead.

I set about working on him, asking God, Jesus, guides and other helpers to pour healing into him. Within ten minutes, the pain had stopped and he felt considerably better but in case he had any internal injuries, I decided to continue giving him healing. After half an hour, I had a rest and asked his father, John, to take over and continue the healing, as he also had healing abilities. We continued praying for light and healing to pour into him for two hours after which I felt sufficiently convinced that he was alright.

The operation had been averted but, of course, with a broken hip, he stayed in hospital for a few days until he could leave using crutches. I gave him healing two and three times a day in hospital. He was permanently surrounded by so many friends all around his bed every day but when I arrived, they all kindly left, knowing what I was doing. It appeared I had the power to empty rooms in a hurry! He recovered well, and has never had any problem with his abdomen or his hip since that time and gets involved in all sorts of sports, triathlons, marathons, rock climbing, skiing and snowboarding.

What was unexpected, however, was when I left the hospital, I was approached by a couple of young doctors who asked me if I could give them healing to quit smoking!

Some Interesting Cases

There can be many reasons for someone's illness and as I developed spiritually, my intuition and psychic ability was opening up. Edward made an appointment to see me and arrived with his neighbour who had driven him. He was 83 years old and was covered all over his body with an angry rash which was bleeding, which he had had for about three years. He told me that his doctor had no idea what was causing it and he was in despair at ever finding relief. I gave him a healing with his neighbour eyeing me carefully the whole time, as though he was intent on protecting him in some way.

At the end of the session, he asked me to send healing to three other people who very badly needed it and he gave me their names and addresses and their complaints. These people had no idea that he was asking for healing to be sent to them.

After a couple of weeks of sending healing twice a day to all four of them, I decided to ring Edward to see how he was. It seemed he was no better and was still scratching and bleeding all over his body. He said he couldn't come again to see me as the transport was difficult so I offered to visit him, he lived about 10 miles away. I felt very strongly that I wanted to help him, as he had been so kind to think of others and arrange for absent healing for them when he was poorly himself.

When I arrived at his home, I found him huddled in the kitchen, wrapped in a blanket, the house was freezing, he had no heating on and it was January. He said he couldn't afford heating. I was appalled. He had a small electric fire on in the kitchen which had warmed that room up a little. I asked him to remove his shirt so that I could see what was going on with his skin. He had three shirts on and they were all stuck together with blood and stuck to his skin. His body was simply covered with a bleeding rash. I took a pot of honey from the cupboard and spread it over his back and chest and then got a clean shirt for him. As I began the healing, this time I picked up that he was extremely allergic to sugar and this was the cause of the problem. He told me he ate lots and lots of cakes. He promised me faithfully that he would stop sugar immediately and would go to the health food shop and buy cakes with no added sugar.

After using the honey on his body, I asked if I could wash my hands but he had no water. His taps didn't work because he had switched the water off, saying he couldn't afford it. He gave me half a tiny cereal bowl of rain water to wash my hands in. At the end of the session, I had been there quite some time and asked if I could use the bathroom. Once again, there was no water to flush the toilet and he followed me up the stairs with a bucket of rain water to pour down the loo, tripped on the stairs and spilt the bucket of water everywhere all down the stair carpet.

By this time, I was so appalled at the way he was living, I sat him down firmly and asked him what on earth was going on and said if he was so hard up, he could claim benefits from the local authority, no pensioner needed to go without heating or water. It seemed he was having the mother of battles with the water authorities at the cost of water and he didn't agree with their charges so he simply turned the water off. He had written to his MP to tell her the water company was ripping him off. I talked to him about getting help and he explained that he was receiving an adequate pension. He had escaped Poland during the war, hung on to the underneath of a train all the way down to Calais in France, and came over to England where he then enlisted with the British army and served the rest of the war for them. He had lived in the UK ever since, working in construction until he retired.

It was good to hear that within a week, his skin had cleared up dramatically and continued to heal until it was back to normal. He then told me he had put my photograph, which he had cut from a newspaper article about my work, on his alter, along with pictures of Jesus and other saints! I insisted that wasn't necessary and he insisted it was!

Skin problems can take a while to clear and with food allergies, an offending substance needs to be avoided for at least 7–8 weeks for it to be completely cleared from the body. I recall the case of a young girl of about eight who I treated, she was also covered in a rash, although nowhere near so bad as Edward's, and that had taken exactly eight weeks to clear.

It is my experience that a lot of elderly people, who have no family, become obsessed with water bills. Mary turned her water off for a year, rummaged in dustbins looking for scraps and dressed like a tramp. She lived in a beautiful spacious Victorian house, which my husband eventually purchased after her death, and when she died, she left almost £300,000 to a cat's home.

Then there was Robert, a very dear friend of a friend of mine. He was 85 and quite badly malnourished. My friend asked me to give him healing without him realising, so I basically prayed for him whilst with him and directed healing to him. He ate very sparingly and he also had a complete phobia about water bills to such an extent, the water board had been around a few times as they thought there must be something wrong. He had a bowl of black filthy water in his sink which he just used over and over again, using it to wash dishes and then wash his underpants. In addition, he saved all his urine and lined up buckets full outside his kitchen door, and used it to 'feed' his flowers and vegetables.

As you can imagine, the smell was unbearable and I wasn't able to spend much time in or around the house and I refused proffered cups of tea, although my friend always partook, praying he wouldn't get E. coli. When I gently offered to clean up for him and suggest he use fresh clean water, as this would be so much healthier for him, he became very cross with me. This gentleman was very intelligent and had great knowledge of wartime, history, vessels and battles, reading avidly. His wife had died after having both legs amputated by a surgeon who said it was necessary to bring down her blood pressure, and he had no children.

He went into hospital for some minor procedure and contracted a hospital infection, lost three stones in weight and went downhill from then onwards. When he eventually died at 86, he had left no will. His brothers, my friend and the lawyer searched the house for weeks. They discovered that, in fact, he had left £1,300,000 plus his house worth £300,000. All this and he wouldn't use any water and bought the cheapest bit of food, usually out of date.

I was asked to visit Marjorie to give her a healing and a friend of hers took me to a farmhouse in the country where this lady of 79 was trying to manage 36 cows and several hundreds of acres of land, with hardly any help. I gave her healing and afterwards, she made us a cup of tea. As she handed me the tea with no milk, I asked if she had some milk to spare and she said no, she didn't have any. I protested that she had 36 cows right outside her back door which I could see and she astonished me by saying that she would never touch any of the milk as the container vats had to be disinfected with such a powerful poisonous chemical, she refused to use it.

What Is Spirituality?

This work has been an amazing journey of spiritual and psychic development, study and spiritual understanding. The journey is ongoing for all of us, as we are learning who we are, why we are here and what we are meant to be doing whilst we are here. This is not our only life, but we have to do our very best with the life we are in at the present time. We need to be free thinkers and contemplate religions and their teachings and only accept what we feel comfortable with.

It is endlessly fascinating to consider religions and spirituality and interesting to see how people think and feel about their beliefs. What amazes me is how fanatical people can be about what they believe is right and wrong, how they can follow scriptures so closely without questioning them and how people can condemn other peoples' beliefs. How on earth can we all profess to know what is the truth and what isn't? Who can stand up and claim they have all the answers?

Our personal experience teaches us more than anything. Once we have personal spiritual experiences, we are in a different realm of understanding, and nothing and nobody can shake us out of it. In order to have spiritual experiences, we can pray, and prayers will give us answers. It may take some time to get the answer, but it will arrive with perseverance. I have had some very powerful answers to my prayers over the years which have astounded me, not only for my own personal needs but also for patients who I am working with. On other occasions, I have had astonishing spiritual experiences which have arrived unexpectedly.

As a child, I went to church with my parents every week and attended Sunday school, and I remember proudly learning prayers by heart. Our local, Church of England, church was 50 yards away, and the vicar and choir slowly and ceremoniously walked around the church, swinging incense and singing mournfully in Latin. I never understood a word of it and barely understood the prayer books, but I had a faith inherited from my parents who knelt down and prayed every night before they went to bed.

A friend came to stay, and until then, I had no idea that our church wasn't the usual Church-of-England-regular-church. We went to church together, and when we left the service, she burst into tears and said it had been awful, that it was a high church, which I had never heard of. The vicar always prayed in Latin, and there was always a procession around the church, spreading swathes of incense. As this was the only church I had attended, it was normal to me. I was simply amazed that she was so upset.

I continued going to church regularly throughout my life. I remember when my marriage had some difficulties, I had a strong desire to be a nun and go into a convent. I met a young lady on my meditation course who had, in fact, been a nun and had come out, and I was very interested in her experiences. It was much later when I saw that I had been a nun in the past life immediately before this one, where those feelings had come from. Right now, I cannot imagine anything worse.

I was in my forties when I discovered something so extraordinary and so devastating that it caused me to have a major spiritual crisis and threw me into turmoil for months.

My Spiritual Crisis

I began to meditate in my early thirties, not long after my mother died, because I was simply not coping with her death at all. I learned Transcendental Meditation, and four years later, I took the Siddha course, which involved advanced techniques, including levitation. Deep meditation brings up all kinds of buried pain and trauma, to be examined and healed. I was astonished at the stuff coming up to be looked at, and it can be very difficult to deal with but is ultimately profoundly healing and beneficial.

Then whilst meditating, I began to regularly see an odd sight in my inner vision; I was seeing the sea, with two boats and someone in the water in the middle. People were looking over the end of the boats at the person in the sea. I noticed that one of these people had a tall, strange hat on. I continued on and off to have this vision for about a year, after which time I decided that I needed help to understand it, as I had no idea what it was about. I, therefore, contacted a friend of mine who was a very powerful healer and asked him if I could have a session with him. I explained what I had been seeing, and he began to give me a healing.

When during the healing, once again, I had this vision, I explained to him what I was seeing, and he told me to hold the vision and then to go in closer and not to be afraid. As I went in closer, I suddenly saw that the person in the sea was myself and that I was drowning. At that point, I had the realisation that the people in the boats were from the church and were drowning me as a 'witch', in a past life. My friend very gently told me to go on a few minutes in time, and I relived the drowning; I was under the sea and the water was black and dark green, and I was truly terrified. Once again, I was gently urged to go forward a few more minutes, when I saw myself rising up and

30

going into white light and seeing many people greeting me on the other side. My healer friend was supporting me and helping me with this very difficult realisation, and I was so badly shaken, he had to hold me and comfort me for quite some time afterwards. When I finally left, I had a drive of about 20 miles home and I had to stop a couple of times to rest.

It is hard to express how this affected me. First of all, I had known nothing about the Inquisition at the time and had only a vague knowledge of 'witches'. To say that I was outraged that I had been drowned by the church is truly the understatement of the century. I was utterly incensed. I was thrown into a heaving turmoil of rage and was completely beside myself. For the first few days, I had to pace around my land, kicking logs and screaming my head off in an attempt to get my anger out. This anger and outrage actually lasted for months. I stopped going to church and swore I would never set foot in another church again. I was very close friends with the vicar of my church at the time, and he visited me and my family at least twice a week; he said it gave him peace and joy to visit us and to get away from all the interfering women in the church bossing him about.

For me, then, to suddenly stop going to church was upsetting for him, and as I did not want to distress him with my news, unsure how he would react, so I just told him I was having a spiritual crisis. Fortunately, he retired six months later and moved about 20 miles away, and although we often met for lunch, when he enquired about the new vicar and how the church was going, I always told him it was fine and going well, although I had no idea as I no longer went.

I took myself along to the library and sat for hours reading about the Inquisition and bought myself books on 'witches'. The shock horror of what the church did has never left me, for they tortured and murdered several million people during the Inquisition; these included any free thinker, anyone who didn't go along with their doctrines, herbalists, healers (witches) and many minority spiritual groups. Their methods of torture and murder can scarcely be believed. In the cases of drowning their victims, if the person drowned, they were then innocent; if they didn't drown, they were guilty, so were murdered anyway. In addition, they had the most unbelievable torture instruments.

I have since 'seen' a second life I had as a healer ('witch') where I was once more murdered and brutally tortured by the church. In both these lives as a 'witch', I have seen myself working and healing people and using a variety of herbs and herbal pastes and concoctions. I was very brave also because I refused to stop working and actually fled from place to place, hiding in different places, knowing that the church was after me. These lives explained why I had a temper, which just went after all this came out.

Having had two lives where I have been tortured and murdered by the church, those fears, however, were buried inside me and are also buried in many thousands of present day healers and alternative practitioners. I recall being quite anxious when moving to Spain, with the fear that the authorities may put me in jail. It was a needless fear from deep within my subconscious as, in fact, the Spanish people are very open to healing and the whole way of life, in many respects, is very laid back.

Pauline

I met a woman when I was nursing and she later became a neighbour of mine. We became friends and I even took her to Spain with me on holiday. However, I began to find our relationship very difficult to cope with because she was constantly criticising me and condemning me as a healer, telling me that healing was the work of the devil, and that her church didn't approve of healers and so on. Strange how churches can disapprove of healers when Jesus was the ultimate healer. He did say after all that what He could do, we could do and more.

I tried to get her to open her eyes to see God in all religions and told her that around 400 million people in the world are Buddhists, and that there are millions of Hindus and Muslims also but she said they were all wrong, believing that only she understood and knew the truth. She was utterly outraged that I was clairvoyant and sadly, her mother would come through many times from the spirit world when I was with her, begging me to give her a message but unfortunately, she would have none of it and said it was utter rubbish.

Finally, I 'saw' our relationship in a past life, where she was actually my torturer in the church, and she took great delight in her duties. I naturally told her nothing about this, but at that point, I realised the friendship had to end and I gently told her that our spiritual differences were too great and I was getting upset. I look back now and am surprised that I was able to remain friends for so long as certainly, now I do not mix with people who are judgmental and spiritually narrow-minded. On learning of our past life connection, I felt we had had unfinished business together, which is why we were thrown together no doubt. I realised I had to forgive her, not only for her judgments and criticisms of my work and beliefs, but also for the appalling treatment I received under her hands in a past life.

In fact, I found it extremely difficult to forgive the church and it took me several years before I could do it. Even then, I practically had to be forced to forgive them by my dear late close friend, Rosemary, with whom I was healing and working in Spain. We met regularly to pray and meditate, and went together to give healings and counselling to various people in the area. Rosemary was, in fact, a pillar of her local Church, the sacrosanct, and had got her priest to bless our meetings and healing work.

One day, whilst we were meditating, the whole subject of the church and the Inquisition came up. Knowing I had to forgive at some time, I struggled with it but with her help and a lot of heart wrenching and crying, I eventually managed it.

Often people ask why it is that they can't see spirits. I ask them if they have ever been involved in spiritual development and in most cases, people have never even considered such an option. Developing spiritual gifts can involve a great deal of work and effort, sitting in spiritual circles, practising meditation, yoga, praying and other practices and these disciplines help to purify the body and mind and gradually develop our other senses. These senses cannot function in a body full of toxins and negative thoughts with our minds purely on money and survival. If we want to develop extra senses, then we need to devote time to spiritual practices. We can all take time to pray for others and the world, and ask that healing be sent to people and places in need, as all our prayers are heard.

It is, therefore, essential that we not only forgive ourselves for whatever we feel we have done or said but also to forgive everybody in our lives who has hurt us in any way. It is also of the utmost importance that we accept our circumstances because I have been told by the spirit world that 'there is a reason for everything'. Therefore, if we have broken relationships, have lost our homes, our jobs or whatever, we somehow have to find our inner peace, no matter what is going on around us. This is our big lesson in life. We need to look at the major problems in our lives and see how we can forgive anybody involved, forgive ourselves and generally accept what has happened to us.

Sarah

There are people who are unable to forgive the smallest things. Someone I know, I will call her Sarah, was unable to forgive her two daughters for sending flowers to her husband's new partner, even though she no longer wanted him herself, they had been discussing separation for some time. She was so outraged that she wrote a horrible letter to her daughters accusing them of betrayal and cut off all communications and as a result, has lost out on their company and the company of her three grandchildren for the rest of her life. She has suffered enormously in the process, crying copiously for years and is filled with such rancour and bitterness that it has affected her heart. She has collapsed several times, has been hospitalised, is taking medication and is on constant alert.

Even after several years, when her daughters tried to make contact, she refused, preferring to hang on to her bitterness and pride whilst constantly referring to their 'betrayal'. She further developed leg problems which are always indications of not being able to move forward. She even went so far as to cut them out of her will and say they were not to attend her funeral. All this because of a bouquet of flowers.

This person was involved in spiritual development and had been giving healing for many years and it really must be said that, we have to do considerable work on ourselves before we can begin to help others. After many years of listening to her telling me how evil her ex-husband and two daughters were, I finally plucked up the courage to quietly suggest she looked at the situation differently and perhaps tried to realise her own responsibility in the matter, and how she could now still mend the situation. Her reaction to my suggestions was extreme; she slammed down the telephone and wrote me an unpleasant letter cutting off all communications. The truth can be very difficult for some people to cope with.

After this, I was shown her inner self symbolically, she was wrapped up with pretty paper and ribbon, a nice outer package and inside I 'saw' her filled with black barbed wire.

There is little point in having heaps of spiritual books, attending churches and talking about God and angels unless we do try and practise some of the teachings we are trying to study.

Obviously, the way we react to anything or anybody is of the utmost importance. Imagine a whole different scenario to the one above. Instead of reacting with such anger and rage and bitterness, she could have sat down calmly and realised it was a perfectly normal thing to do, to send flowers, and she could have let it go. She could have been pleased that her husband had found some happiness after their 35 years of unhappiness together. She could have wished him well and sent him love.

I have noticed that a person who cannot forgive someone usually cannot forgive anyone. This same lady Sarah, was having a consultation with me some years ago and her father from the spirit world came through to speak to her, as sometimes happens. She claimed to have had an unhappy childhood saying her father was cold. On this occasion he asked for her forgiveness, knowing what she thought, explaining that he hadn't realised he had treated her coldly, and really did the best within his understanding at that time. She went very quiet and as the mediator, I asked her how she felt and would she like to tell him there and then that she forgave him. Silence ensued and finally she said no, I cannot forgive him.

Frankly, I was shocked, it is not easy for a spirit to come through to speak to us and it is a blessing when they can and do. Here was a perfect opportunity for healing this relationship and for forgiveness to occur. If we cannot forgive someone, it is possible that we will be born again to experience this relationship once more and reach the same point again, where we need to forgive this person. So, what is the point of hanging on to old grievances, it does the spirit no good at all.

About a year later, during another consultation with Sarah the same thing occurred, but this time both her mother and father appeared. They both asked her forgiveness and once more, after a few minutes thought, she refused. After the session, I tried to gently ask her why she hadn't taken the opportunity to forgive them and she replied that she was unable to. Three years after this, the situation was exactly the same, saying she was still trying to forgive them. So this lady continues to go through life hating her parents, hating her ex-husband, hating her children and breaking her heart because she is lonely and feels she is a victim of what life has dealt her. She said so many times, 'why should I apologise' to my daughters? In addition, she obviously could not forgive me for trying to get her to see things in a different way.

What a way to go through life and yet so many people choose to behave in this way, not realising the damage they do to themselves. I have been shocked on many occasions with people who claim to be spiritual, participate in spiritual development, even give healings and yet cannot even get on with their own families.

For God's Sake, Let's Forgive Everybody

Pride is often the reason for the lack of forgiveness, an inability to apologise or reach out to someone. Sorry can be hard to say but that word can be deeply healing. I have often said sorry even when I really believe the situation wasn't my fault; I would prefer to end an uneasy feeling and I have found then that the other person will also apologise but didn't have the ability to say sorry first. I would personally prefer to be humble than be in agony over discord.

It seems that forgiveness for some people is almost impossible to do and yet I can so vividly remember the scene of devastation in Ireland after a particular bombing some years ago, when a father cradled his dying daughter in his arms and said he forgave the people who had killed her. I, along with millions of others, was moved beyond words.

We all react sometimes too quickly so if we could take some deep breaths and before picking up pen and paper or telephone, we sleep on the problem for a few nights and then see how we feel. If we have begun to practise forgiveness already, then it gets easier and easier to do every time. Eventually, we may be able to reach a point where we can forgive everybody for everything, whatever it is, in our own world and in the world in general. A tall order but a goal worth striving towards and one I believe we are all meant to learn.

As we know, forgiveness is a fundamental element of spirituality and all religions. Forgiveness involves our souls, our spirit, our very being; it is our test on this earth and we need to embrace it completely. There are spiritual laws operating in our worlds and all my studies into these matters have taught me that love and forgiveness are the two most important issues to learn in our lives on earth.

We need to get started straight away, there is no time to lose, and make a powerful effort to take time out and do whatever is necessary to forgive anybody in our life who has hurt us. It not only frees them, it frees us, liberates us and empowers us; it removes the negative emotions within us and then there is space for love, health and happiness

Let's all forgive everybody, including ourselves, bless our past and all we did, forgive ourselves for all the terrible things we think we did, said and thought and move on. Let's forgive everybody in our lives for all the hurt they caused us, all the things they did to us and said to us, how they treated us, and let them go, wish them well and let's move into a world of thought that is full of love, gentleness, joy, happiness and peace. A tall order for someone whose mind is a whirlpool of negativity at the moment, but take the first step and improvement will gradually come about.

Imagine the difference in our lives then if we deliberately send thoughts of love, forgiveness, compassion and healing. Imagine if we could forgive all the people in our lives who have hurt us and send them love. Everybody benefits. We benefit and they benefit, clouds of pain and upsets can dissolve, our auras will be cleaner and we can feel lighter, they will feel better without realising why, and we can get on with our lives in a clearer and more positive state.

So many people have said to me that they can never forgive someone and they do not realise that the only person suffering in that scenario is themselves, by hanging on to these detrimental thoughts, they alone are causing themselves harm. If you feel it is impossible to forgive someone, then pray for help, take time out and ask whoever you feel comfortable to ask, God, Jesus, angels or whatever spiritual guidance you may choose, and sit quietly for some time with eyes closed and calling on this help, try then to forgive. Take time to go through your whole life and see who needs forgiving, not forgetting yourself. Get help from a good healer if you find it too difficult to do on your own.

It is not always the easiest thing to do but if the person is no longer in our lives, we can try to forgive them for what they may have done and then just let them go. The reward for forgiveness is happiness and peace of mind – when you have these qualities in your life, your life changes beyond belief; your life is filled with joy and love and you find yourself smiling and laughing easily and often. Give yourself time, if you have a lot of people to forgive, give yourself plenty of time to go through them, one by one. When you can send the person love, wish them happiness and really feel that you mean it, then forgiveness will have taken place.

Mary

I stayed in touch for many years with a school friend I will call Mary: who lived near us at home and after her first divorce, she remarried a widower. His wife, after the birth of their third child, had committed suicide by lying on some railway lines. Mary and Peter then went on to have a further child of their own. One Christmas, Mary overheard her three stepchildren criticising her in another room and she told me she went berserk. She threw all three children out into the street; they were aged around 12, 14 and 15. I was so horrified when I heard this that I was reeling. I expressed my feelings strongly and tried to convince her that this was an outrageous thing to do and that she should not have done it but she was adamant, she would not put up with being criticized. The children had no money and I cannot imagine how they managed. They had grandparents in a town about 100 miles away and I presume they must have made their way there somehow. As a result of this, I had to back away from this friendship, although we spoke occasionally on the phone and she and her husband visited me in Spain.

To this day, and about 30 years have passed, they have had no contact with these children. I have tried on a few occasions to suggest that she forgive them and try to find them and make it up to them for all they must have suffered, but to no avail. So, not only did they lose their mother in a horrendous way, they also lost their father who appeared to do nothing about the situation at all, and their so-called new 'mother'. It is worth mentioning that Mary had fallen out with her sister when she was 21 and has never spoken to her since and her sister had fallen out with their father before he died. The last conversation we had some years ago, I suggested that unless she made up with all these people in this life, she would have to go through it all again in another life. She said nothing on earth would convince her to make up with any of them. In one of the spiritual development groups I run, this lady's father came through to us from the spirit world on three occasions expressing his deep dismay at what had happened.

This kind of situation cannot make anybody happy. Inside, nobody will ever find any peace of mind or happiness with such circumstances. As a couple, they now spend all their money on themselves, travelling the world on cruises and although this may bring some superficial pleasure, deep down there will be a great deal of suffering, as our conscience doesn't leave us in peace.

Avoiding Negative People

Personally, I have had to back away from negative people. They can take our energy and leave us depressed and exhausted. The more sensitive we become, the more we need to clear and protect ourselves. Instead of seeing the beauty around us or appreciating their blessings, a lot of people only concentrate on what they think they haven't got. Many years of healings and nursing very sick and often bedridden people taught me to be grateful for everything in my life, my mobility, my sight and the beauty around me.

As we become more spiritual, we develop our sensitivity and can then detect what is false, and I have found it to be a revelation and truly shocking 'seeing' certain people. I have been utterly amazed to 'see' people, whom I previously thought were gentle and calm individuals, as a bundle of rage and resentments underneath, like raging infernos, full of jealousy, hatred, bitterness and rancour.

With increased sensitivity one starts to see the internal state of people's emotions and the truth about people and situations. Black swirling energies within a person can cause severe health problems, often to the heart. If the chakras become really black, a person can die.

Eileen

I gave regular healing over a couple of years to a lady with multiple ailments, including blindness. This lady is intelligent and has a strong mind and manages to use her computer, order her shopping and arrange her life without sight and with very little mobility, maintaining her sense of humour at the same time. She further has managed a long distant friendship, and travels by train and plane. Her house is in chaos with piles of stuff everywhere but she knows more or less where everything is and nobody is allowed to move anything. She manages very well to organise her life and her many hospital appointments, and the last thing she wants is sympathy.

Occasionally, I would arrive at her home feeling a bit fed up about something trivial but when I left and stepped outside, I was just so utterly grateful that I could see the beautiful green grass, the trees, the flowers, the neighbours passing, the blue sky, the cats sunbathing. I relished my ability to walk down the street with ease. We so often take these things for granted and don't even notice them.

Family Relationships

Even our own families and close friends can shock us. Someone, who I thought of until recently as calm and happy with her life, flabbergasted me a while ago. Something occurred which caused me to 'see' her, she is a mass of tangles of resentment with the way her life has gone, deep rooted anger and bitterness inside, whilst portraying calm outwardly and often saying how happy she is. Bravado and pride can cover up a mess inside. This mess has affected her heart and nerves very badly.

So many people have difficult relationships, and there are many things we can do. Sending love to a person or persons can greatly help, and we can pray for help and see white light pouring into them; this can bring about the healing of emotions. We can picture an entire family surrounded with light. Also, we can call on various spiritual beings for help with the healing of any relationship, such as Jesus, Mother Mary and in particular Archangel Raguel who greatly assists with all kinds of relationships.

We must not allow others to disrespect us in any way. If we do, this is handing them power. If it is some sort of gentle constructive advice, then that is different. When we are powerful, others putting us down and dishing out unnecessary criticism will not make the slightest difference to us. We can see ourselves rising above difficult situations.

We need to learn that we only need our own approval; other people's approval is not needed or necessary. Their disapproval cannot affect us. Most people are yearning for other people's approval, but we need to reach a place where we totally love and approve of ourselves to such an extent that we are utterly comfortable with ourselves and do not need approval from anybody else at all.

Internal Chaos

Clearing out traumas and negative thinking can take time; it cannot all be done at once, one thing at a time needs dealing with. Sometimes we aren't even aware it is there. Meditation brings stuff up for us to look at and then deal with. I have been practising Transcendental Meditation since 1975 and became a Siddha in 1979, which involves levitation. I was astonished at how much stuff buried inside me surfaced over time and once all that was dealt with, past life upsets surfaced. It may not sound like much fun, looking at upsetting events, but unless we do, the soul carries these burdens from life to life, in addition to having deep negative effects on us in this present life. Furthermore, the body itself can carry these burdens and make us ill.

I recall an incident when I lived in Spain where I was attacked and injured by a woman, in front of a crowd of people in the village square. She took me so much by surprise, beating me with a wooden pole, that it took me a few minutes to start to defend myself. Also, she was older than me and I didn't want to hurt her. Next day, I was covered in bruises over my face, around my eyes and on various parts of my body. You can imagine that I was stunned and also humiliated. I have documented the story in my book *Calamares and Corruption*. After I had recovered from the shock, a couple of days later, I sat down and sent her love and forgiveness, and did this a few times. I didn't want this festering inside me.

What I didn't know was that although I was saying and thinking the words love and forgiveness, the incident had gone inside me and got lodged. About three years later, something triggered off the memory of it whilst I was driving my car and a tumultuous eruption of rage within me came to the surface and I had to pull off the road; fortunately, I was in a remote place in the mountains. I then shouted and screamed my head off and punched the passenger seat with my fist over and over until I got my anger out, this took me about 20 minutes until my hands hurt and my throat was parched! This rage took me by surprise, having thought I had forgiven her long since. It taught me that sometimes we are not aware of the anger we have inside us. When I had calmed down, some while later, I then sent the love and forgiveness that was necessary and that was then the end of it, I had finally got over the incident.

When a person is full of anger, resentment, rage and bitterness, there is no room in there for anything else. There is no room for love, peace, appreciation, happiness, joy and laughter. One cannot function in a peaceful and organised way full of negativity. Negative emotions literally consume and strangle us.

Certainly, people don't want to be around us if we moan. Once we can make that transition from feeling loss and lack in our lives, and start realising how much we really do have, we begin to change. The purpose of our lives on this planet is our spiritual development; this will mean self-awareness which can be painful. It is so much easier to blame others for our predicaments rather than take responsibility for ourselves to think in different ways.

This is why it is important to clear it, get this stuff out, look at it, let it go, send love, forgive people, forgive situations, punch pillows to get rage out, scream and shout somewhere, have therapy and have healing. It's worthwhile to read spiritual books, understand we need to accept our circumstances whatever they may be, know that we have many blessings which we can appreciate and also recognise the fact that most people are doing their best according to their knowledge and understanding.

A Profound Need to Protect Ourselves

Whereas it had been normal for a long time for me to 'see' clients and their problems, illnesses or negativity inside them; it has to be said that 'seeing' so many negative emotions in someone who I had previously thought was gentle and spiritual was a shock for me and after a couple of incidents involving people close to me, for a while I doubted my ability to assess someone's character. I felt deceived and unnerved by their outward appearances and although we are trying not to judge, there is a need to assess people around us for our own protection, as there are many needy people about, who simply suck our strength and who have hidden agendas.

In the early days, I began to notice feeling ill in public places and having to leave shops and towns when I had only just arrived. In one shop, I actually collapsed and discovered later that somebody had been murdered there. At first, I wasn't sure what was going on but devouring books on these subjects, I soon learned how to protect myself. The more we develop and the more sensitive we become, the greater need for this protection. If it is forgotten, the negative effects from other people can be profound. People with dark and negative energies can affect us very badly, and make us ill and unbalanced. I have also taught my three children how to protect themselves.

The very first experience I had of this effect was when I volunteered in court to help a family in my village. I was to be a mediator in taking care of a small child of four years old, whilst the father visited for one hour every week for 12 months. This man had recently come out of jail for having sexually abused one of his other children. I spent the hour constantly vigilant, and never for one moment letting the child out of my sight. After the hour was up, I felt abnormally exhausted and had to go and lie down, often falling asleep and this was in the afternoon. At first, I thought this reaction had been caused by the sheer strain of the situation. However, after two or three visits with the same result, I realised that this man's energy was severely affecting me.

The more sensitive we become, the greater the need to practise methods of protection for ourselves from everybody, including difficult family members. We can see ourselves with an eggshell shape of white light around us and as we progress, we may need more protection. I surround myself with three layers of gold light, three of silver light and three of purple light. I ask Archangel Michael to clear my energies every night when I go to bed and ask for protection night and morning and extra protection before going out, near crowds, sick or negative people.

Also, healers need to take special care to protect themselves because patients can keep thinking about us and cause attachments which can take our energies and deplete us, without us realising it. Also when someone is depressed, desperate, or lonely, they can be sending out thoughts unconsciously but, in fact, causing attachments or ties. It is essential that we try to learn how to 'see' these attachments.

A member of one of my yoga classes confessed to me one day that she was sending me rage, hate and bitterness; I was utterly astonished and asked her why, and she said it was jealousy and she wanted to be like me. She was a beautiful young girl with long blond curly hair, and I had been helping her in many ways and even gave her cat healing at 1 a.m. after an evening of work; when I would have preferred to go home to bed at that time. She said she had been making dolls of me and my dog and sticking pins in them, and as my dog had recently collapsed and died in the woods on a walk with a heart attack, I was truly horrified.

I cleared all this away and surrounded myself and my family with protection, and sent her love, forgiveness and healing. Sometime later, she was admitted to a psychiatric hospital after dropping her new born baby on its head as it was the wrong sex, and I was called in after a couple of months to help her. She hadn't spoken for two months and nobody could get her to say a word. The healings I gave her there helped her considerably and she began to speak and eventually recovered.

In serious cases such as above, we need to also surround our home and surround their home, to stop the hate and rage coming out to us and twice a day surround ourselves with the white, gold, silver and purple protection, both to us and our properties. Also pray that all the negativity be taken down into the ground and ask spirit to transmute it all into white light.

These negative energies will so badly affect the person experiencing them that their chakras – the spiritual centres throughout the body – will have huge patches of black, the aura will have black and grey clouds, the internal organs will be filled with the effects of these negative emotions and illness can be the result. It is, therefore, very important that we clear our auras and protect ourselves. We can often forget and I recall someone staying in our house for a few days who was quite ill, and afterwards I felt really rather poorly but could not pinpoint the reason. I had forgotten to protect myself and when I could not recover from this feeling of malaise, I 'looked' and 'saw' that I had a black attachment which seemed embedded. It was unintentionally put there by a very strong need for help from this person, towards me as a healer. I asked for spirit help and it was removed from me, and I immediately felt much better.

Ties are invisible cords which connect us to other people, and cutting these ties can be very therapeutic; it can release the stranglehold that some people may have over us, which allows us to be who we are meant to be and liberates us from being held back. Powerful ties can come about by people wanting to control us or have a desperate neediness. It has to be said that these people do not necessarily realise that they are sending forth cords but this is how powerful thoughts can affect us.

In many of my counselling sessions, I have been able to see ties between my client and someone else and help them cut and free themselves. I have seen very powerful strangling ties which are literally preventing someone from moving ahead with their lives. If you sit quietly and close your eyes and ask for help to see, you may be able to see a tie yourself, see who it is connected to and cut it. Imagine pulling these cords from both yourself and the other person and then imagine them being thrown onto a bonfire and burnt. If you are unable to do so, it would be useful to have a good healer to help you. We can have ties to various people and they can also be deeply connected from past lives.

Thoughts Are What Change Our Lives

They are our nucleus, the basis of our being and we all need to check what we are thinking. We've all heard of positive thinking but it has so much more of a powerful effect than we imagine. What we think about others will affect ourselves, what we send out comes back to us, so therefore, if we have loving thoughts about other people, this love will benefit them and ourselves. We can go several steps further and have loving and positive thoughts about the world and everybody in it, as negative and despairing thoughts do nothing whatever to help.

I am often very surprised at the bad state people can get themselves into when in fact, they aren't really ill and do not have any real problems. So many people get depressed about such trivial concerns and make their own lives unnecessarily difficult. As hard as it is to accept, many cases of depression can be self-pity. Often when we can see this, it can turn us around completely. Some people will feel angry that they could be suffering from self-pity and think it is totally untrue. I know people who never stop moaning about almost everything and it seems never to occur to them to actually concentrate on their blessings instead, to appreciate the home they have, the bed they sleep in, the family they have around them, the food in their fridges, the beautiful trees and flowers in the world.

If we can reach a point where, as we are beginning to feel miserable or we get up feeling down or fed up, we grasp our thoughts by the scruff of the neck and say – no, I will not think like this, I will try to see the beauty and positive aspects of my life. Sometimes I get gently tough with people on this issue because they have thought so negatively for so long, have wallowed in self-pity and misery for so many years, they have no idea how to go about seeing their lives in a different way.

There are endless books in the market about positive thinking and repeating positive statements all day long, is a great way to start. I remember when I first began to say I love myself and I approve of myself, I actually found it quite difficult as I didn't agree. However, these affirmations when repeated over and over sink into the subconscious and, eventually, bring about great changes. It cannot happen overnight; these principles are life changing and take time to be effective. We need to concentrate on our strengths and also frequently remember all our achievements and the kindnesses we have shown others.

The alternative is to continue wallowing in negative and damaging thoughts, and this traps us in the dung heap. What we think is what comes about so if we choose to continue thinking how we have messed up our lives, how we have hurt our family, how we made a wrong decision, how we could have done things better, how we let someone down, we just remain stuck going round and round in the quagmire of negative thoughts.

A simple knack of getting out of negative thinking, worry, anxiety and endless chewing over of problems is to deliberately make the mind concentrate on something beautiful, healthy and positive, such as our successes no matter how small, and the wonderful qualities we like in other people and ourselves. For anyone not used to the self-discipline of meditation, a quiet ten minutes with the eyes closed thinking of beautiful countryside, trees, rivers and mountains can help calm the mind and, gradually, begin the elimination of lower energies.

We need to realise that at the end of our lives, we take only our spiritual qualities with us to the next world. It is great to have material success, but it is also essential to have spiritual success in peace of mind and behaving kindly to others.

After a particular period of aggravation in my life with a variety of irritating problems, I was shown by spirit to imagine myself rising above them, seeing myself riding a winged unicorn, flying above it all and looking down, and from above, these problems can look petty and simply not worth worrying about. If you are having a hard time with a member of your family or some other person, take some time to quieten the mind and be still. Try to sense your heart opening, and send love to the person or persons and situation and then see yourself rising above it all, this has a liberating effect.

For our peace of mind, we need to detach from world affairs, wars, cruelty and destruction. This principle applies to family aggravation and any other problem you care to mention. Otherwise, we are in a constant state of agitation about something or the other. We must rise above them and not give the problems or the people aggravating us, any power whatsoever to upset or disturb us. The state of peace of mind is the ultimate goal for all this work and that peace is utter bliss. This does not mean that we do not care. The way we can help to bring about peace is to pray and ask for love and healing to be sent to anyone who needs it, we can ask angels to surround any situation in the world, and also try to see the world in a positive way, as this then helps the world to become more positive.

Healing

As healers, we are channels through which divine light and healing pass into the client. Over the years, I have given healing to hundreds of people. Each client is different and I discovered that there are people who appear to enjoy being ill. There are also people who simply refuse to help themselves and just expect the healer to do all the work for them. Some people are simply lonely, bored or do not have enough to occupy them, and they dwell unnecessarily on every twinge.

Giving healing to people can be very frustrating at times. In general, most people are grateful, understanding and receptive. However, there are people who don't listen, refuse to understand anything you say, and don't even bother to say thank you at the end of a session.

Iris

Iris, a lady farmer, came for a few weeks dressed from head to toe in black. She was very depressed and miserable and said they had gone bankrupt but it turned out that they still owned several properties and many hundreds of acres of land. Her only concerns in life seemed to be money. I suggested that she wore pastel colours, blues and greens, as these colours would help the healing. She took no notice and came each week in black. I suggested the same thing again one day and the following week she arrived in mostly black with a bright red jumper. Colours do affect us, red can make us angry and irritable, and black can certainly make us depressed.

One day she rang me and urgently asked me to send healing to a bullock that had fallen down in the ice and was stuck in the freezing cold. I asked her why she wanted healing for this animal and she told me that if he died, she would lose £500. I promised her that I would send healing and I prayed for the animal and also that if it died, he would do so peacefully. The bullock had died before we had even finished speaking and she was naturally upset about losing her money.

Doreen

Living in the country, I am surrounded by farmers and one day Doreen, an elderly lady, came for healing and greatly benefited. However, whilst discussing food, I told her I am a vegetarian and she became very angry and said that she and her husband were totally anti vegetarians, which I have to confess I found quite amusing. She later developed food allergies and again she was helped.

Angela

Angela came regularly for a long time receiving healing but would never do anything to help herself. She was constantly having problems related to vitamin and iron deficiencies and I always seemed to be suggesting she ate organic fresh vegetables and organic foods. I even did food allergy testing and deficiency tests on her and she assured me she was following the suggestions from my diet sheets. Then one day, something she said indicated to me that she was taking no notice whatsoever. She just wanted to sit there, receive healing and not lift a finger to help herself in any way. I wasn't very pleased and I told her as gently as I could manage that she really needed to make some effort to change her diet in addition to receiving healing but she was most displeased. In fact, she didn't come back for healing for a year!

It is so often the case that simple remedies can heal so many complaints but people seem to have lost this knowledge which was known and used in days gone by.

As we progress spiritually, and the more we meditate, pray, devote our time to spiritual practices and study, there comes about a gradual awareness of our spirit connections of guidance and help and this is truly a joy. It is what all healers long for, to see and hear guidance. Inner vision is invaluable when healing patients.

Jose

Jose was a tiny very thin man who came for healing in Spain, seriously worried about his weight and his health. As I began working on him, I 'saw' dozens of worms and knew immediately that these were the cause of his problems. When I finished the healing, I gently told him what I had seen and advised him to take raw garlic and also to take some medicine which I knew was available in chemists. The poor man was very embarrassed but worms can affect people quite easily, especially in hot countries where there are a lot of insects. We give our horses and dogs fresh garlic regularly to keep them free of worms. There is however controversy now about giving garlic to dogs so only very small amounts are advisable. To avoid intestinal parasites, it is recommended to wash hands after touching all animals and before preparing food.

Past Life Therapy

Very early on with my healing work, it took an interesting turn when during a session, I suddenly started seeing an entire scene before my eyes of what was obviously my client in a past life. At first, I was unsure whether to mention it but it was too powerful and clear, and it seemed most definitely necessary to tell her. She was naturally fascinated and, of course, what I was seeing was related to her present problems and we were able to throw light on them and give her a greater understanding. However, the session then continued for two and a half hours whereas a normal healing usually lasts no more than an hour.

After a few such sessions like this, I realised that I needed to separate the two therapies, as it was also proving difficult to concentrate on the healing itself. Past life therapy can greatly help clients who have persistent problems, which are difficult to understand. Sometimes the cause of emotional and even physical problems can be rooted in past events, which we have experienced in previous lives, and we have brought traces of these problems into this present life. This therapy can also be beneficial in understanding ourselves and our relationships, our abilities and interests.

Bringing past experiences out into the open can help us understand what is going on in our lives and we can use various methods to heal them. I have seen so many interesting and also painful past lives. The most prominent people in our lives, at the present time, have been with us before and possibly many times. Some past lives I have seen have been gentle or fairly normal, but some have been very traumatic. This therapy is a very powerful healing of the soul.

Some past life sessions.

Here I will give a few accounts of some of what I have seen.

Helga

During one of the Alternative Medicine Exhibitions in Marbella, Spain, where I had a stand, many people wanted healings, past life readings and food allergy tests. A Dutch lady approached me and asked for healing. We went to a private room and she told me that she had chronic insomnia and had hardly slept her whole life. I began, as always, by placing my hands on her shoulders and doing my usual prayers before I started and straight away, a vivid scene unfolded.

I saw a prison camp which I instinctively knew was in Germany during the last war, and barricaded behind barbed wire was a yard with a few people about and several guards patrolling with Alsatian dogs. Then I saw my client as a young girl about 13 years old and as she stood to the side of the yard, a guard released two dogs to set upon her and they flew across the yard and brutally savaged her to death. I have since read that this was quite a common occurrence. It was very shocking to see and I was also trying to understand how this could have been the case when this lady was 50 at the time. I was then told that she had been born again six months later.

As this was such a traumatic vision, I waited until the end of the healing and then gently explained what I had seen. I then asked her when she was born, and she confirmed that she had been born during the war. She also told me that she was absolutely terrified of dogs and had appalling nightmares of being attacked by them and simply hated German people. Her feelings were so powerfully strong because she had been born again so quickly after this harrowing death. She joined my meditation/spiritual development group in Fuengirola and one evening, we were joined by a German lady. As soon as she sat down, my Dutch client jumped up shrieking that she could not share the room with a German and rushed off down the street, with me running after her.

She came to me regularly for a further six months and we worked through all these problems. She found it very hard to forgive. Gradually, she began to heal and finally was able to sleep at night with no nightmares.

Janet

As I began working on Janet, I saw she had a huge black tree-like coil up through and between her legs and out the top of her head, attached to a past life, where she was a gypsy in Ireland, she slept with someone else's husband and a curse was put on her. This was done 200 years ago and was still with her. In this case, we worked through this, cutting ties and banishing the curse put on her using prayers. Then later, I saw a past life where she had put a knife through her own heart, because of her lonely life; living in isolation in a tiny house in the middle of nowhere, she had nobody, and decided to end it all. These sessions can be very traumatic but they are deeply beneficial.

Barbara

Barbara came to me with great loneliness; she was in her late 50s and had only ever had one brief relationship when she was young. I saw her in a life in Canada where she was married and living with her husband in a pleasant house. Then I saw her packing a suitcase and walking out the door, and she just carried on walking down this very long road. Her husband was heartbroken and never really recovered. She had just upped and left with no word of why, and it seemed that she had just been bored with her married life. Obviously, with a case like this, I then tried to help by offering positive affirmations and prayers to comfort her and hopefully change her life for the better.

Anna

A whole group of people booked me up for several days, and arrived from Wales in a small bus to stay in my area. Some needed healing and others wanted past life therapy. One of the ladies, Anna, was unable to conceive and had many other problems, and I was rather perturbed to see a past life where she was practising black magic. In fact, she and many others had done a great deal of harm to a lot of people, including murder, and I saw a lot of unpleasant things I would have preferred not to see. I was worried about telling her any of this and very much played it down, leaving out many gruesome details. I recommended that she learnt to meditate and pray for others and the world, knowing that this would help to shift some of her karma.

Rebecca

On a much lighter note, Rebecca, a very pretty elegant young Spanish lady who had a stand next to mine at one of the Alternative Medicine Exhibitions, asked me for a past life reading. We didn't have much time but we had a lull in the proceedings and I linked in with her and saw quite a sight. She was in Japan about 2000 years ago, dressed in the most bizarre clothes, huge foot ware of materials wrapped around her feet that looked like they were made of leather and rags. She was wearing many layers of rags and strange head coverings and wandering the countryside with a companion as a tinker. It was a very strong image but it seemed so incongruous to her present day life, it caused us a lot of amusement.

Of course, people can worry about what they may have done in their past lives, as obviously in the normal way we are not aware of them. One gentleman came to me for a reading and said if he had killed or harmed Jesus, please don't tell him! I was relieved to see that he hadn't and gave him a past life reading which was quite innocuous. The way we can lessen what karma we have is to live peacefully, be loving and kind, be forgiving, and pray for others and the world and give back in whatever way we can, by helping and caring.

This very morning as I write, I had been sending prayers to heal the world and as I finished, the room was filled with beautiful golden and mauve lights, indicating that spirit had heard my prayers. When I pray for the world I see it as a globe as though from a distance, and I ask for white light and love to pour into everywhere and ask for dark negative energies to be cast off. I see black pouring from the world and ask that it be transmuted into white light. I pray for light to pour into all war zones and places in need.

Many clients have been fascinated to learn certain facts, for instance, I saw one lady who had been a wonderful singer in a past life and when I told her, she confirmed that she was a singer in this life too. These details are good for me to hear too as it brings confirmation. We bring over our talents and abilities from past lives and then usually develop them further. Exceptional talent such as well-known musicians will have developed their abilities in possibly many previous lives. This does explain why some people are quite brilliant in their fields.

Healing Animals

Animals and birds make good patients as they do not resist or disbelieve. I have been called on to give healing to so many animals and birds over the years. When I lived in Spain, all the local children would hammer on my door with a cat, dog or bird that needed attention.

A Peregrine Falcon Fledgling

One time, the children were very excited and begged me to come outside and they took me to a large bird that was face down and splattered on the ground with wings outspread. It looked as though it might be dead but I put my hands just above it and said my usual prayer and immediately it pulled in its wings and slowly sat up looking most confused. It was an instant healing which was really amazing.

It was a big bird but young, a beautiful peregrine falcon; it had obviously fallen from its nest from the top of our extremely tall church. We took it indoors and it perched on a shelf, and I fed it with cooked chicken on the end of a fork. It ate well and thrived, and seemed perfectly happy in its new surroundings, but after a week I contacted a bird sanctuary who came and collected it in order to then teach it to hunt and fend for itself.

Molly the Moorhen

One Christmas, my family and I set off to my sister's for Boxing Day and on the journey, just near a river, the car in front of us hit a moorhen which was crossing the road. It was lying by the side of the road and I insisted that we stopped to check if it was still alive, and I picked it up and put it on my lap in the car, blood was pouring out of both eyes and there didn't seem much hope. However, I immediately asked for healing and the bleeding stopped and he settled down, and when we arrived at my sister's, we found a box and some hay and found some worms, bread and water. My brother-in-law kept peering in the box saying I was quite mad to expect it to survive and he simply didn't believe that its eyes had been bleeding.

Well we had a good day, lots of us playing the piano and having a lovely meal, and we took the moorhen home and he lived in my study for a week, recovering and eating very well. After this week, I decided he could go back home and we all drove the 35 miles or so back to the same spot where we found him and gently placed him on the riverbank away from the road. He hurried off full of energy foraging for food and I felt very happy knowing that his recovery was a miracle. My sister afterwards wondered if he had told his family and friends that he had had a very nice Boxing Day with much feasting and music!

Our Beautiful Boxer, Sophie

When our boxer dog Sophie was very young, one or two years of age, she started frothing at the mouth and having fits. I took her to the vet who referred her to Langford Veterinary College at Bristol University. There she was wired up to machines in a laboratory and they discovered five heart defects. These included a very swollen heart muscle, a leaking heart valve and an ectopic heart beat (an extra beat).

They gave me some tablets for her to take and told me to return in a month. I did this and took her back, they rewired her to all their machines and she was exactly the same as before. They then said they didn't know what else to give her and that I was to keep on with the tablets for a further six weeks and then return.

I got home, threw the tablets in the dustbin and began adding various heart-healing ingredients to her diet. I hadn't begun to do healing by laying on of hands at that time so this was purely diet. I mixed a handful of pure wheat germ into her food every day, a large spoon of various herbs and rosehips, which are healing for the heart. I begged and stole as many rosehips from anywhere I could find them and in the hedgerows, and I also added rosehip syrup to her diet.

Six weeks later, I took her back to Langford. Five vets in their white coats put her back on the table and wired her up again. I was very nervous. After some time, the head guy came over and said we cannot understand it, she is completely cured. What did you do? I told him and he wrote it all down. They were all utterly amazed.

Camelot, Our Beautiful Horse

A very powerful healing took place on Camelot, a beautiful massive 13-year-old, 18 hands horse my daughter had received as a birthday present from her husband. After riding him, he developed a huge, very swollen fetlock. I gave him about three healings on this over a couple of weeks and the swelling gradually went down, leaving him with a slight swelling which he seems to have always had, and did have when Rachael bought him. The previous owner said he had always had this injury. Rachael, when buying him thought that she would be able to sort this out somehow.

However, during the healings, I was told by my inner guidance that this horse was utterly and completely worn out; his muscles, body and his strength. His previous owner, an 18 stone man, had hunted him and ridden him to the point of exhaustion. As I tuned into him, I was told that, in fact, he had been ridden almost to death sometimes, that he was overworked then neglected, overworked and then neglected, over and over. In other words, he was simply used for hunting time and time again, and when that was over, he was then left to his own devices, turned out in the field and ignored. The vet, in fact, confirmed that the tests on the fluid in his joints confirmed that he had been worked terribly hard.

I felt quite alarmed and angry with his previous owner by what I was hearing, and wondered how we would get him back to normal strength and health. I did a test on his diet and we determined the foods and supplements he needed to eat to regain his strength. I had recommended to Rachael that she rested him thoroughly and didn't ride him at all.

However, not long afterwards, thinking that a short ride wouldn't harm him, after only a few minutes, Rachael had to get off him as he faltered badly and she had difficulty in walking him back to the stable. Very worried, she called me to give him another healing and fortunately, this time, she was unable to be there with me. I began this healing in his stable which was knee deep in straw and with nobody else around I was able to concentrate properly. On previous occasions, I had had various people crowding round, wanting to know what I was doing and talking the whole time.

As the healing progressed, I began to see jagged shafts of light pouring into all his muscles, like shafts of lightening, which I had never seen before. About half an hour into the healing, Camelot's eyes began to glaze over and he looked as though he was going into a trance. He became very tired and droopy and then to my surprise, he went down on his knees right there with me in front of his head, and then lay down, desperately trying to hold his head up. He then placed his chin on the straw and unable to stay awake another moment, laid down completely flat on his side. He grunted and whimpered a few times and then fell fast asleep.

I have to confess to being a bit unnerved by this, horses do not normally lay down in front of anyone and I was greatly relieved that my daughter wasn't there as she could well have panicked and called the vet in a fright! I knew from experience that healings can be very powerful and can make people and animals very tired sometimes and I calmly tried to keep my faith. However, it was extraordinary that such a reaction had taken place and I continued to give him healing for a few more minutes and then decided to stop. I sat with him by his head on the straw for a further half an hour watching him carefully and then I decided to gently touch his forehead and wake him up. He was in a very deep sleep and he slowly came around, looking quite dazed, shook his head, stood up and then said, "OK, I'm fine, where's my lunch?"

I rang my daughter who was, fortunately, busy and couldn't get there to panic! She confirmed that it was most unusual for a horse to lie down in front of someone. I knew that this horse had had a very profound healing indeed, and I wondered how it had affected him internally. A test I did a week or so later confirmed that he was very much better.

A short time afterwards, I received a call from my daughter saying that Camelot is a completely different horse. He has an energy that he didn't have before; he is alive, happy, alert, excited and full of beans. He is still the same sweet, well-behaved animal but just so different in himself. He has come to life and my daughter is riding him gently. He is full of joy and strength. I was also told that it would take a year of good care and careful riding before he was back to full strength. However, the difference in him already is down to the amazing power of healing, of that there is no doubt. My son's reaction on hearing the story was, "Wow, fancy flooring a two storey horse! Can you send me some that?"

What a shame that some people treat their horses like bicycles, to be used and dumped as though they have no feelings. Then when they are tired of them, sell them on like a used car or put them down.

Horse Show

I recall an incident many years ago, when I was at a horse show where Rachael was competing on our horse Tammy, and a horse there collapsed. Panic set in and people were running about shouting and ringing the vet. I quietly ignored them, knelt down beside the animal and began to give him healing. The owner, a large rude farmer, was hysterical and he and others were shouting at me to get back in case the horse stood up, but I just ignored them. I quietly carried on healing for about 10 minutes after which the horse stood up, shook himself and appeared to be perfectly alright. It wasn't until another 20 minutes that the vet arrived. The owner didn't even have the grace or manners to thank me and nobody around even spoke to me. I was simply stared at. After the event, however, a couple did approach me and ask for healing for their own horse.

As a healer, I have come across so much opposition, disbelief, scorn and downright contempt sometimes. It amazes me how closed-minded people can be and how they can dismiss something so utterly, when they have no understanding of it whatsoever. How is it that life and the human body can be so magical and such an amazing feat of complicated wonder, and yet people cannot open their minds to the possibilities of miracles. Religion also often blocks understanding.

May, a 7-Year-Old Mare

This case has just occurred this week as I write. It is an extraordinary case, May, a magnificent grey horse had been shaking her head wildly for some weeks and wouldn't allow her owner, Emma, to touch her around the head or put a head collar on. Three different vets had been called out to May, and none of them could find anything wrong with her. She rang me in a very agitated state saying that the mare was going to be put down in a week or so. She said I was her last hope, which is often the case with healing work.

When I arrived at the stables, I asked the owner to leave me alone with May for about half an hour, as I find I can concentrate so much better without anxious people around me. I then began the healing and an inner voice was telling me straight away that she had ear mites. I checked every inch of her head and neck, as obviously Emma's fears were that the mare had a tumour. All was well until I reached her ears and I discovered they were not only sensitive, but very dirty. I picked up without any shadow of doubt that she had a bad case of ear mites.

I advised Emma to put a small amount of pure unrefined virgin olive oil in a bowl, about a tablespoon, then chop up a fresh clove of garlic, add to the oil and leave this to soak for at least a couple of hours. Then strain a little of oil through a tea strainer and put a few drops into each of the horse's ears and massage the ears to make sure if reaches all areas. This remedy kills ear mites instantly. The garlic should be left in the oil and if necessary, use a few more drops of this mixture the following day. The same remedy works perfectly with cats and dogs also.

The following day, the horse was already better. She put a few more drops into each ear to make sure and after two days, the horse was no longer shaking her head. At the time of writing, Emma is very angry with the vets and is talking about suing them. She is also, of course, overjoyed that her horse is better and there is nothing seriously wrong with her.

Sienna

One of my daughter's horses was calling out to me one day during my meditation and I went to see her, we knew she had been badly treated before we had her, and I picked up that she had been bullied and shouted at whilst out walking and throughout all her earlier life. When we got her, we could hardly get near her, she was so afraid; it took us a long time and lots of patience for her to trust us. I gave her a long healing and afterwards she was so much calmer. I felt her pain welling up as the energy poured into her and it made me cry.

Communicating with Elementals

We can go outside and ask nature spirits to help us with whatever problems we are struggling with. Whilst meditating in the garden, I was surrounded with a cocoon of white light. The spirits around me informed me that I was receiving very deep healing of the cells of my body. I was told that each cell of the body is affected by everything, our experiences, past lives, pains, happiness, emotions and thinking. Every cell. As we clear ourselves of negative thoughts, our cells begin to clear and get healthier. A lot of stuff is gathered into each cell from past experiences, way back to times when we are unaware. There is deep-rooted stuff locked into the cells which need to be sorted out. I was told that this is what this deep healing and cocoon of light was doing. I asked why I still have a couple of health problems

First of all, I was told not to believe you have these conditions; you don't acknowledge them or give them space. You simply don't acknowledge them. You don't say or think you have them, because if you do, then these thoughts cement themselves into the cells and become reality. This is why it is so important for people not to talk about illness or their illnesses because they are then compounding and anchoring the illness in their body.

As you have more and more joy and positive thoughts, the cells begin to clear and heal themselves and this goes on more and more. It is very deep and complicated; a huge amount of data and information is stored in each cell, and all our experiences are found there. This is why it is so important to have therapy, forgive, clear, let go, embrace the present, find the joy, find the love, find the blessings in your life, love one another and do your best. Holding on to bitterness, hate, rage, regret, loss, pain, suffering, jealousies and any other negative thoughts simply embeds these conditions into the cell, into all the cells, and causes blockages and this in turn causes illnesses.

It has to be said that as we progress spiritually and our bodies become clearer and purer, then a lot of foods become unacceptable to the body. We then have to make sure we eat organic foods and take great care in the foods we consume.

Fiona

One of my clients was in a very bad state. As I began the healing, I saw that her heart was blocked by a shield, and I was confused and asked, "What is going on?" I was told to prepare myself for what I was going to see. As I hadn't experienced this before, I felt nervous and braced myself. I then saw a sword through her heart, a terrible metal pin at her throat and scissors at her forehead. The shadow and memory of these were from a past life where she had been tortured by the church during the Inquisition for practising healing.

I saw metal spikes in her heart, again shadows from the torture. In addition, I saw a dozen black ties to her heart from people around her needing her. I had never seen such a bad case.

Then I saw her lower chakras were all grey and black. In this case, the client was living in a difficult situation with the people around her deeply needing her love, due to the death of a loved one. She had no energy and wanted to cry all day. She could not cope and was feeling utterly suffocated. She needed so much healing.

During the healing, I set to clearing all these attachments and psychic wounds. I asked for the highest source of light and love to pour into Fiona to remove all these effects and blockages. I call on Archangel Michael in cases of clearing but also ask for Jesus to help and for any other powerful being to assist. I called on Archangel Raphael who works with healers. I asked for all the black ties from people around her to be cut and removed. Then I saw the instruments and effects of the torture leaving the body and the body filling with white and emerald green light. I ask for white, green and gold light to pour into the body and aura. I taught her the yogic alternate nostril breath, and also taught her how to meditate. At a later date, I checked this client and her body was completely healed and clear of all past life traumas and ties to those around her.

When people around us or even ourselves are extremely needy, it can form an attachment which can deplete the body's energies. These ties need cutting and removing. We can do this ourselves during meditation, or we can request the help of a healer capable of this work.

Powerful past life experiences are brought over into present lives, and can severely hamper our progress and happiness. If you doubt the tortures from the Inquisition, I recommend checking relevant books in your local library. When I lived in Spain, there was an exhibition in Malaga of the horrendous and unbelievable torture instruments used in that time by the church.

There are many present day healers, herbalists and alternative medicine therapists, who have these instruments of torture or memories still embedded in their aura. These memories can affect our mental and physical health without us realising it. The church tracked down and hounded anybody practising natural medicine and anyone with alternative beliefs, then tortured them, drowned them, burned them alive and murdered them in any way they saw fit. About three million people were destroyed.

Yoga

Yoga is a very powerful practice which heals body, mind and soul. It heals the internal organs, heals nerves, is calming and brings about great peace of mind. I taught yoga for 20 years, and for most people it is purely a physical exercise class. Although it certainly is this, yoga is a far more potent discipline which when practised regularly will awaken spiritual awareness and have very deep and positive benefits. It can, of course, be practised purely as exercise, but a good teacher will go into the spiritual effects. These benefits occur in any case.

There were many cases of people being healed by yoga during the years I was teaching. A wonderful lady joined one of my classes and she was, by then, about 65 years old. She was slim, fit and healthy. I encouraged the class to share with us any positive feedback they may have regarding self-healing, and this lady inspired us by telling us that she had been crippled with arthritis for many years and doctors had told her she would end up in a wheelchair. She decided firmly that this was not going to happen, and took up yoga. In a few months, her arthritis had gone and here she was in front of us, a picture of health.

A couple of years ago, I developed sciatica which was very painful and caused me to limp a little. As I was very busy, I didn't stop to think about doing yoga postures. Eventually, I sat on the floor and did the appropriate yoga postures for 10 minutes, and I was completely cured. Yoga really can be magical.

A young man, who joined one of my classes, began because he had not been able to work for some months due to a severe back problem; he had been told he had an extra vertebra which was causing him a great deal of pain. In a short while, a matter of a few sessions, his back problem was completely cured and he was very impressed. He enjoyed the classes and became very keen and proficient.

After a couple of years, he suddenly found God and became intensely religious. He had returned to his native South Africa on holiday and a family member had told him that yoga was an evil practice and he should stop it immediately. I reassured him that this was not the case but his uncle was involved in a fanatical Christian group and finally, he came to see me at home, gave me a very hard time and told me that what I was teaching was evil and I should stop immediately. We had quite a fight about it, and I told him, in no uncertain terms, that he should get down on his knees and thank Jesus for the yoga which had opened up his spirituality.

Unfortunately, I have come across this kind of attitude from many others, often very narrow-minded Christian fringe groups and other religious groups. I do not allow it to affect me in any way. Having been handed a leaflet at my door by another religious group who called often, informing me about the evils of yoga; the next time they called, I informed them that I was a yoga teacher. They left very quickly and thankfully never returned.

There are church vicars who will not allow yoga to be practised in their halls. I was fortunate not to have this problem. To condemn yoga is simply ignorance. I recently read an article in a Sunday newspaper written by a Catholic priest who announced that yoga was very dangerous as it leads to Hinduism, which is evil. I was utterly appalled and horrified. People condemn practices that they simply do not understand, usually from fear of the unknown. If we could all only understand that there is one God but many pathways up the mountain to the top, if we could only all be tolerant of each other's beliefs and stop trying to tell everyone else what to believe, the world would be such a happier place.

During my meditations, I am always being urged to do more yoga and I have been very privileged to be visited on many occasions from the spirit world by Yogananda, Sri Yukteswar and Babaji, wonderful Hindu saints. I have also been very blessed to see and receive personal messages from Maharishi Mahesh Yogi, the founder of Transcendental Meditation, which I have explained later in the book. These visitations and messages have been very deeply moving, uplifting and encouraging, and I am extremely grateful.

A Snail's Pace

I have one client whose spiritual progress is like a snail, she is someone who doesn't listen, and despite various vitamin deficiencies, still refused to eat salads and green vegetables. During consultations, I could see her system was very sluggish and during one session, I was told that unless this person follows the advice, healing would be greatly diminished. She wasn't very pleased and it took so long for her to heed the dietary advice.

An incident occurred around her, where a stray cat arrived at her home and she refused to feed it or let it in her home. Fortunately, a neighbour started to feed it but the animal still had to sleep in a shed. During a reading with this client, I was told that the cat had been sent to her to help, heal her and for the cat also to be healed. She has a large spacious home and she could easily have taken the cat in. She refused and during this reading, I was told that her spiritual progress is very slow and that she should try and overcome her stubbornness. We are honoured that spirit come close to help and guide us. Animals, of course, are capable of healing us and cats are taken into hospitals and put on patients' beds for that purpose.

Coping with Difficult Relationships

As we progress spiritually, we develop our sensitivity and awareness and can see the truth in situations. We have the ability to tune in, meditate and ask and sense what is happening, and this can be extremely helpful, in helping ourselves to cope with situations and difficult people.

But what is important to realise is as we progress, clear ourselves of past traumas, open up to God more and more, purify our bodies, minds and thoughts, we are then unable to be around people who are vibrating on much lower energies. This is why we have to walk away from certain people because they, in fact, can be harming us by contaminating us. Our vibrations clash.

In fact, I have noticed from my own experience that some people around us are actually removed in ways which are definite but peaceful. The more we progress spiritually, the more people seem to be removed. This can be alarming but if we have faith, we will soon see that we are then surrounded by people on much higher vibrations; people who are more loving and more sensitive.

When it comes to our families, this can be much harder to accept and when we are trying to be spiritual, loving and forgiving, having members of our family being unpleasant, angry, full of hate and rage and generally thoroughly difficult, what do we do then? I had to ask my guides and helpers in the spirit world because I have had this very problem with members of my family. I was told to detach from the drama, stand back, rise above it, send love, send forgiveness, pray for their happiness and 'let them go'.

I was told to pray for self-awareness to begin in these people which was of slight concern to me; however, I believe it is essential and also important for their growth. I have been told that I am a catalyst and channel to change other peoples' level of consciousness. I have noticed that one of them is now talking about forgiveness and not judging, although isn't practising it. In quiet moments when we are alone, we can say the following to people who have deeply hurt us in the past.

I forgive you and let you go. No more, that is it. You no longer have permission to mistreat me, I wish you love and happiness, and I let you go into the hands of God and love and I am free. I forgive you for all your treatment to me all my life, and I am now totally free. We can say this, write it or shout it loudly. This is an excellent way to deal with difficult and controlling, vindictive and impossible families.

There are a lot of dysfunctional families out there with controlling parents and partners. I recall a client with an advanced state of cancer when she first came to me. Her mother had told her she was ill because she hadn't had children, the mother had caused her untold pain and suffering, laying a big guilt trip on her, nagging her for years to have children. I gave her exercises to cut ties from her mother as she was dragging her down so much. This lady received healings for a few weeks which greatly relieved her pain and stress but she passed away at the age of 39. Sometimes, in cases of advanced stages of disease, where the disease is too wide spread, healing can help to alleviate pain and anxiety and help them to pass over in peace.

Hilary

Referring to the case of my client Hilary, who I mentioned at the beginning of the book, we had a number of consultations in order to try and heal the bitterness she felt towards her parents. Throughout several sessions, I was able to communicate with her parents in the spirit world and act as an intermediary between them and my client.

When Hilary was 19, her mother had been living abroad for a while and the father went to visit. After the father left, the mother committed suicide. At a later time, when they were alone together, her father wanted Hilary and him to both commit suicide. Her father attempted suicide on the motorway. A nightmare family life.

In one of our consultations, when I was communicating with her parents in the spirit world, Hilary poured her heart out to them. Her parents were sad, downcast and ashamed. Hilary was on one side of me and her parents on the other, Jesus Christ in the middle. He just appeared. I wasn't expecting him, but he does come in very deep healings. But then, I never know what is going to happen until we start. She was told to talk about her childhood and how she felt, and tell her parents what they did to her – which was very heavy, the mother threatened her with a knife, she drank, would change moods and become like a different person. Hilary would run off to the next farm and stay away for hours and was afraid to go home. Her mother would tell her she wanted to kill her and it was all her fault because she had behaved badly, which was untrue.

Jesus had his hands on all of them, his right arm over Hilary and the other arm over her parents. He poured light into all of them. In my client, the whole of her lower self from waist to base was dark – black and grey. This was all removed and sent down into the earth.

The conversations were very moving and her parents were both deeply sorry for the way they had treated Hilary and begged her forgiveness. They were appalled and ashamed at how they had treated her and the effect it had had on her. The mother especially was very remorseful at having taken her own life, and had been in the shadows of the spirit world for a long time. Over a number of sessions, my client was able to forgive her parents and they were overjoyed by this. With the light and healing sent to the parents in the spirit world, the mother was able to come out of the shadows and be reunited with her husband.

I saw light pouring into all of them. Their grief was all cleared, and I was told that all their karma was finished, that they were all free of each other now, as forgiveness and apologies had occurred on several occasions. They had had centuries of connections through karma. It is all gone. This is a very powerful soul level healing; it frees the soul and everybody is able to continue on their path. They were deeply grateful that they were able to communicate in this way and that they had found peace together.

At the end of the session, her parents sent their love to Hilary, thanked me, asked again for forgiveness from her, and walked away, saying they could now progress spiritually in the spirit world, as all this stuff had been holding them back. They said they wouldn't leave her, they would be there for her if she needed them and that they continued to love her. We both thanked Jesus for his help and the extraordinary healing that had taken place. A very powerful healing indeed.

After this particular session, Hilary was interested to learn about the laws of karma. I gave her some examples of karma relating to relationships and past lives, and how we need to work through different issues with them. She rang next day to say she found it so difficult to believe that Jesus Christ was with us, although she believes me, it seems too incredible for her to take in. I told her that He comes to me often and I have seen him many times, that he helps me with very difficult and deep healings.

One point here to note is that in Hilary's case, all the powerful emotional turmoil had been lodged in the lower part of her body from the solar plexus down; the solar plexus does involve emotional problems and appeared to have affected the lower three chakras. However, hate and rage can affect the heart as I have seen in various clients. In Hilary's case, she didn't feel hate and rage, just sadness. Each case is different and each case will affect the body in different ways. I see different things with different people.

Alice

I remember a case in Spain of Alice, a young woman in her thirties, who came with her family to see me when I had a stand at an Alternative Medicine Exhibition in Marbella. She was very sad and asked for a healing, and as I put my hands on her, I saw long cords which went up, and attached to her parents in the spirit world. She told me that they had been both killed in a car crash 10 years before and she just couldn't get over it. I told her she needed to let go of them as they couldn't progress in the spirit world and she would remain unhappy, and that she should concentrate on her husband and two children. She said she couldn't. She left as unhappy as she arrived.

Many people are not interested in advice and sometimes we have to stand back and let people get on with everything and just concentrate on our own spiritual development and work. What does simply amaze me is that most people just run to the doctor for the slightest thing, even headaches, stomach aches, they don't make any effort to sort things out themselves, instead give their own power away by expecting someone else to know how to cure them.

Even healers do this; they don't try and see where the illness is coming from or how they could best serve themselves – perhaps with self-healing, prayers, fasting, diets, etc. I had a healer recently come to me for healing; she was unable to walk, in a lot of pain, had great difficulty in getting up the stairs, said she would come regularly, came once and never came back, even though the pain reduced considerably during the consultation. She knew nothing about chakras, or how the colours of the chakras changed.

A Very Negative Client

We do have to be careful of people who suck the life out of us. I had a client who I was seeing regularly every week, but still she felt the need to ring me in between our sessions and talk for nearly an hour about all her problems, illnesses and relationships, and what all the doctors and specialists had to say. She talks of nothing but illness, there is no other subject in her life of any interest to her, and therefore, she is one mass of illnesses. She was even cross with me because it had taken her some time to get through to me on the phone. She was another person who would not improve her diet or take any exercise. The last phone call of this duration, I decided would be the last. It is hard to get through to some people when they are so negative.

A client has to make some effort to change within themselves so that healing can take place; they cannot just sit there and expect to receive healing and do nothing for themselves. It is essential to become aware of our thoughts and the words we speak. I am no longer prepared to give healing to anyone who is not willing to help themselves, by changing the way they think and speak or by changing their diet if necessary.

Those who talk about illness all the time attract illness to them. People who keep saying their parents had certain illnesses so they too are bound to inherit them, will end up with them because that is what they fear or believe and therefore, that is what they will attract. The power of the mind is utterly extraordinary and it is extremely important for us to become aware of our thoughts and words. In order to be well, happy and successful, we must be vigilant.

It seems that whatever we think and say, we vibrate at that level, so people who resent others, those who live in the past, those full of regrets, who cannot forgive or forget, who fear illness, death and loss are attracting other people with the same mindsets and are attracting all kinds of mishaps and negative conditions to themselves.

If we examine our thoughts very carefully, we will be astonished at the number of people we resent or to whom we feel some kind of antipathy. It can be due to simple things, stuff we have locked in, feelings towards people for minor events in the past maybe, whatever we think they have done or not done, we need to urgently forgive them and send them love and wish them all joy and happiness. Feelings of resentment can be directed at neighbours; maybe they are parking badly, getting on your nerves, ignoring you, or worse even causing you severe stress.

Neighbours from Hell

Many years ago, in an upstairs flat, I had some extremely unpleasant and difficult neighbours downstairs. They complained about me endlessly, if I ever played my piano during the day, they would bang on the ceiling or hammer on my door. I packed piles of carpet under the piano but this didn't help. I finally gave up playing. They complained about the shoes I wore and said I made a noise. They had a huge dog that pooped all over their garden and they didn't pick any of it up so the smell was awful and I had to walk a path through their garden to get to my front door and try hard not to tread in all the enormous piles of mess.

One day, taking the advice of another neighbour, I put some soil on top of some of the poo on the path to make it look a bit more pleasant and keep the smell down. The guy then threw the poo all around my garden and over my table and chairs, then tried to smash my door in and threatened me with violence, telling me he had already served a jail sentence for GBH. I was so frightened I had to call the police. They both shouted and constantly used bad language and one way and another, it was an utter nightmare. Trying to talk pleasantly to them got me nowhere and I reached the point of utter despair. It went on for months and was making me ill. I just could not work out why I was having to experience all this nor how to cope with it.

My son was very angry and suggested he came down from London with some friends to sort them out, but I know he had in mind more than a pleasant conversation and I knew that would not be a good idea.

It finally occurred to me to send them love! Looking back now, I cannot imagine why I hadn't thought of it before but sometimes when we are mired into a difficult situation, we cannot see a way out. I remember my son thought I had lost the plot when I told him what I was going to do – but I am a healer and do deal with love and forgiveness after all, and it seemed the only possible solution. I decided to spend some time every day, sat in a meditative position, pouring love and healing downstairs and filling up their flat. I carefully devoted time each day and asked my guides and angels to help me. I imagined their flat being cleansed, all negativity being removed and saw it filling first with white light from the highest source, then golden light from the angelic realm, then emerald green light from Archangel Raphael to bring them healing.

About a week later, the guy was hammering on my door again, once more in a very belligerent mood, screaming at me and accusing me of cutting the wires to his Sky connection. Instead of being afraid, as I had been, I decided to send him love as I looked at him and when he had finished ranting, I quietly said I had no idea what he was talking about or where his wires were. He showed me the damage and I assured him that I wouldn't dream of doing such a thing, and that I wouldn't harm anyone or anyone's things. I very quietly told him that I was a healer and I carefully picked up every slug or snail on all the paths and put them in the hedges so that they wouldn't get hurt.

His reaction utterly astonished me. He suddenly broke down and holding his head in his hands, apologised profusely to me for the way he had treated me, the way he had verbally abused me and threatened me, said he was deeply sorry for nearly smashing my door in and swearing at me. I said, "Don't worry," but before I could continue, he said in a very anguished state,

"But I do worry, I do worry, I am terrible, I lose my temper and don't mean it, I say awful things and really regret them afterwards." I told him again not to worry, it was all OK, and in an effort to calm him down and help him, I told him that when I was young I used to have a bad temper but I cured it by learning to meditate. I suggested he do the same, as it would no doubt help him. He then said if I ever needed any help at all, he would gladly offer his assistance.

The relief with this encounter was immense and from that moment on, we smiled and chatted pleasantly and all was well.

They even started to pick up all the dog's mess every day. Then, even more miraculously, they moved shortly after this exchange and new and very pleasant neighbours moved in!

There is, no doubt whatsoever, that the love I sent them brought about this dramatic change, and within only a few days. It was obviously a lesson I had to learn. If we try to apply this principle to any situation we are struggling with, any person we are having difficulty with, good results will ensue. We must remember, however, that only love, healing and forgiveness should be sent.

Then, again, some neighbours opposite to me who have about five cars were parking outside in what was supposed to be my immediate neighbour's and my parking places, and it was getting on our nerves as we had to park way down the street. I decided to stop moaning about it with my friend next door and send love to the culprit instead, and within two days, the problem was resolved.

Any harm or bad thoughts we send anyone will return to us and cause us many problems. If we wish other people to suffer, we will suffer ourselves. I knew someone who practised as a healer and told me that she was having neighbour problems and she actually deliberately sent harmful thoughts. When she saw the look on my face, she confessed to knowing that this was wrong. I felt that she of all people should have known this. I was truly horrified, as this amounts to black magic and can only harm the sender. I did of course realise that this particular healer was in a very low vibrational state and completely deluded about her energies. It is a good idea to check out a healer, if at all possible, before embarking on any consultations.

If everybody could only grasp the fact that what we send out is what we get back. It only harms us if we criticise and judge people. Moaning keeps us locked into lower vibrations and we will attract people who moan and criticise. Lower vibrations attract similar vibrations and will never bring us happiness. In fact, when we are operating on these low frequencies, it is not only people of a similar kind that we attract but all sorts of things can go wrong with our lives.

None of this is easy to those who have barely begun with these concepts, but if we can concentrate on our blessings, be thankful for them and think of all we have instead of what we don't have, we will make great headway.

As we progress mentally, emotionally and spiritually with this work, we will find that some people around us will leave our lives, because the more positive and loving we become, the less we are able to cope with negative people. It is not only people around us that change, our attitudes change, we become happier and in fact, our whole world will change for the better

I think as human beings, we understand so little about how we are affected, how we function, and the effects of people and events around us. A constant barrage of depressing news on TV about wars and murders is extremely damaging to us, and there is no need for us to listen to all this stuff day after day. Getting into a rage about politics certainly doesn't improve our health. It is better for us to spend some time each day sending love, healing and prayers to war zones and people who need help: the world, animals, forests, rivers, seas and the earth itself.

Wonderful prayers can be sent to all leaders and members of all governments in the world asking that their hearts and souls be filled with love and compassion. This is a far more beneficial and powerful way to deal with these things and certainly something that every healer and caring person will want to do. The more people doing this will bring about much greater effect.

A wonderful benefit of developing spiritually, healing ourselves, clearing out all our negativity, is that we begin to 'see' the truth about others and situations. Once this begins to happen, it helps us enormously. We can begin to see why people behave the way they do and at least make allowances for them, instead of condemning them.

The Miracle of Tammy

Our horse Tammy, aged 31, who we had had since she was nine years old, now 34 years old as I write this, was knocked down in the road on 2 March 2004, and sustained four fractured bones in her front left leg, mainly around her elbow joint. She was in intense pain and it was two hours before I knew about it and got to her. She was so bad; I thought she may die right there and then in the road, she had stood back up from the ground but was swaying and we had to prop her up with bales of straw to try and prevent her falling down again. I called the vet who came out and gave her a painkilling injection. She was unable to walk and the road was blocked for several hours.

Friends at the stables rallied around to help us and we backed a horsebox up to her and managed to load her and take her to the vet's where she had X-rays. The normal course for a horse with broken or fractured bones in the leg is to put them down. I found a strength I hadn't known I had before and firmly informed everybody that she would not be put down and insisted that I would heal her. We got her back to her own stable and I embarked on the daunting task of giving her healings, whilst being surrounded by gloom and despair. Nobody believed that I could heal her, including my own family. The vet put her on a sufficient dose of painkiller that took away the worst of the pain but still enabled her to feel it so that she would not put too much weight on her leg. She had to be tethered fairly closely so that she could not lie down.

After the first healing which I gave her immediately on the road, she began to eat the straw which was preventing her falling, and with the help of the painkillers, from the word go, she seemed to be bright and cheerful and continued to eat normally. Within one week, I had three powerful dreams telling me that I had a lot of hard work but would have a big success at the end. These dreams helped me enormously, especially in the face of the disbelief around me. My only support was a client and friend of mine who knew that healing works and she sat with me on many occasions.

I sat with Tammy from early morning until evening every day, virtually camped out for several weeks at the stables, going home only to sleep. I gave her three healings a day, each healing lasting half an hour. I prayed to God and asked Jesus, Archangel Raphael, St Francis of Assisi, Maeve and any other angel, Archangel, vets or surgeons in the spirit world who could possibly help to heal her. I also applied a poultice of the herb comfrey, which can be called knit-bone.

I envisaged the white light of Christ and the emerald green light of Archangel Raphael filling the whole leg. These colours would change, however, and different colours would flood in. At each healing session, there were at least two or three angels around her.

She appeared to be doing very well and her leg seemed to be getting stronger. Then after three weeks, we had a major setback. The vet had warned that there could be serious problems when the injuries would reach their weakest point after about two weeks, when the muscles would separate from the bones. This point had arrived after three weeks and the vet confirmed that her fears had materialised. She said that the bones would now not mend because at the elbow joint, two lots of muscles were pulling in different directions and pulling the bones apart. Her words were, "I won't put her down today but you need to prepare yourselves for that over the next two weeks."

Again, I insisted I would heal her. I was not prepared to give up. An extraordinary strength seemed to be with me, especially with nobody around me believing it. Various people and neighbours would peer over the stable door with such pity on their faces as they thought me totally deluded. My daughter thought I was just blanking out the inevitable, and was seriously worried about how she would ever get me through the trauma.

Ten days later, she put weight on her leg in the stable. I actually 'saw' the moment she was healed. During the night when I could not sleep, I sent her absent healing and this particular night, I saw her in the stable surrounded by about a dozen shadowy figures, everything was dark except for Tammy's front leg which was a brilliant silvery white light. I then saw someone bend down and sew the muscles and bones together with what looked like ligament. I knew at that moment, she was healed. She had to be tied up in her stable so that she would not lie down in case she couldn't stand up again, and although I had seen her being healed and she was putting her leg on the ground, I was nervous of untying her.

A couple of days later, some noise startled her whilst I was with her, and she pulled her head sharply and the rope broke and she fell down. I got such a shock but she just stood straight back up again. I tied her again, still very nervous. Just a while later, she pulled again and fell once more to the ground, (knee deep in straw I might add) and this time a loud voice told me in no uncertain terms to have faith, she is healed.

It took four and a half weeks from start to completion. As soon as we let her out into her paddock, she took off at a canter and it was a wonderful sight to behold; it made us cry. We still have our beautiful horse in our lives, we have had her for 26 years and she is part of the family and the sweetest horse in the world. She moved to Spain with us for eight years and has had all kinds of adventures. Tammy was nine when we bought her and my daughter Rachael was 10. She joined the pony club and did lots of jumping with her, cross-country and dressage, and won 59 rosettes with her over the years. I have always ridden her myself too and we have had wonderful rides over Exmoor, Devon in England and in the Andalucían mountains together.

It was an extremely distressing roller coaster of emotions which left me traumatised by the experience. However, healing a 31-year-old horse of four leg fractures is an incredible miracle and I am overwhelmed with gratitude to have been given this spiritual gift which has saved her life.

Meditation

As we progress spiritually, with working on ourselves, practising meditation and yoga, praying for the world and becoming more and more positive in our thoughts and deeds, many astonishing things can occur.

Probably, one of the most extraordinary occurrences is the beginning of Kundalini energy awakening in the body. Almost nobody has the faintest concept of what this means, not even yoga teachers. I taught yoga for 20 years and even though I had read about Kundalini energy, had discussed it in my classes and had some knowledge in how it supposedly functioned, I wasn't really aware of whether or not I was experiencing it.

I began practising yoga in 1973 to try and help myself recover from my mother's death. Two years later, although fitter, more supple and somewhat calmer, I was still in desperate need of help and in 1975, I began to practise Transcendental Meditation. Four years later in 1979, after also losing my dear father, I began the advanced meditation technique of the TM Siddhis programme, which includes levitation. I practised these techniques of meditation very seriously and spent hours meditating, even though I had three children and we were running a thriving business from home, had loads of animals and so much stuff was going on in our lives. I just somehow insisted on fitting it in, no matter what time of the day or night.

These advanced techniques of meditation are very powerful and bring up all kinds of buried traumas and upsets we have experienced in our lives, in order to air and heal them. It is a long process which can also be very painful as we are forced to look at things we would prefer to forget. When the process has cleaned up masses of problems from this life, past lives start surfacing to deal with! Although it sounds traumatic, buried negative emotions need to be healed otherwise our health is affected. Furthermore, we can never be full of joy whilst we have all this stuff stuck inside ourselves.

Learning the advanced TM Siddhis meditation programme took many weeks. The first part took place over a period of several weeks and in fact, was conducted in my home, which at the time was a beautiful detached house in the country which my husband and I had built ourselves with the largest kitchen to accommodate rows of chairs and the privacy necessary to conduct this procedure.

The house was wired so that each person was attached to a separate telephone connection. Via this connection, we received instruction from Maharishi Mahesh Yogi, the founder of the Transcendental meditation movement, and the teaching came in from Switzerland. We would follow the meditation instructions given until the next session, where we received further tuition. Our teacher and organiser who had arranged these sessions was very concerned with privacy, and we had to black out our windows because at the time we had allowed a pilot to keep his three small aeroplanes on our land and he was regularly walking past the kitchen windows! At the end of these teachings, for the second and final part, we then had a further two weeks' full-time course in a beautiful country mansion.

This final course involved learning levitation. The levitation was simply the final part of the deep and powerful meditation process. Those two weeks were extremely interesting. Men and women were separated into groups of about 25 in each group. We were put into large and beautiful rooms with the floors covered with deep foam mattresses. We then hoped that during those two weeks we would be able to 'take off' or 'fly' as it is sometimes referred to. You may be able to imagine that it was very amusing and much laughter took place. After about three days, whilst deeply meditating with eyes closed and sat in the full yogic lotus position, I lifted off into the air and landed on a girl in front me. It simply happened. There is no coercion, no forcing and trying. It simply happens when the system becomes clear enough. Some people on the course didn't take off at all.

An Astonishing Happening

During those two weeks, I was either laughing or crying. It was a time of huge emotional upheaval.

My mother and father had died not long before this, also my father-in-law and my best friend who had had a car accident and been in a coma for six months. I had a very happy childhood and my parents were wonderful. We had a very loving relationship and I had already done a great deal of crying about them all over the years but one night on this course, I simply could not stop crying; I cried the whole night long about them all, grieving and simply unable to accept that they were no longer with me. I had prayed for some years to see my parents so that I could be comforted and also to know that they were still around me. This particular night, I prayed this prayer constantly because I felt in such pain. By 7 a.m., I was utterly exhausted but certainly completely unable to sleep.

Then something utterly extraordinary happened. I was too exhausted to go down to breakfast and had been lying on my side utterly spent for some time facing the windows which were huge, gazing at the sky, feeling very drained and listless. The sky was blue without a cloud to be seen anywhere. I then suddenly noticed that small clusters of white fluffy clouds were gathering into a shape and this shape entirely filled the window I was looking at. That shape was my mother's face. To say I was astonished is an understatement. As I looked in wonder at my mother's very clear and unmistakeable face, it gradually cleared and was replaced again with small clusters of white cloud forming, this time came the face of my father, again filling the entire window so that it was huge and very clear. Once I had seen it clearly, it again faded and this time, the window filled with the face of my father-in-law. When this faded, the clouds formed again into the face of my dear late friend. After this faded, the unmistakeable face of Jesus Christ appeared and filled my window.

It is difficult to describe how I felt; I was simply, completely overcome and overwhelmed to the point of stupefaction. I lay there for a further two hours, never once taking my eyes from the window or the sky, in case something else should appear, but I had had my prayers answered and so there was nothing else to show me. I stayed in my room for several hours and didn't join in any meditation groups or meals until later in the evening, when I went down to dinner. A few people asked me what was wrong but I didn't tell them anything about it.

In fact, I only told my husband, my brother and my local vicar, who was a good friend of mine. I was overcome with emotion discussing my vision with them. I could not speak about it to anyone else for a further two years. I eventually told my yoga classes when I was able to control myself sufficiently without tears. The vision helped me enormously, it comforted me, supported me, proved to me that prayers will be answered if we keep on expecting them to be.

I have read a beautiful account, by Paramahansa Yogananda; the author of *Autobiography of a Yogi* where he too was deeply grieving for his mother after she passed away, and he was berating God for taking her and how was he supposed to live without her, and he too prayed to see her and, in fact, saw her several times in the flesh sat next to him, which must have been wonderful.

Another Extraordinary Experience

This occurred when with some friends, I went to Mentmore Towers in England for the day, which at that time was owned by the Transcendental meditation movement and where Maharishi was conducting a conference. One thousand people congregated there and we all meditated together; once again, women and men were separated. Group meditation is very powerful as it involves quantum physics, meaning that the power created hugely exceeds the energies of the number of people participating. In addition, we had the presence of Maharishi.

Afterwards, I left the meditation area and joined a friend of mine outside in a small square. He and I seemed to be in a different state and we were dancing with joy. For a week afterwards, I was in a state I had never before experienced and never since. I was in a state of joy, of bliss or wonderment. I guess this state is what human beings are meant to reach eventually. Every person I met seemed to be beautiful, the world appeared magical, I remember being in my garden and looking at the flowers and grass and each plant seemed to be a miracle, each blade of grass quite wondrous. Unfortunately, after a week of this extraordinary unusual state of being, I returned to normal.

My own personal experience with meditating with a large group of people was varied, I seemed to be the only one suddenly seeing swirling colours, angels and spirits and I felt uncomfortable, and also unnerved as to why these things were happening to me and not to those around me. I began to keep quiet about what I was seeing and hearing and after some years of group meditation with other transcendental meditators, I had to back away and continue alone and with other groups as my experiences were becoming too different.

Powerful meditation can affect us in many ways, we can feel light headed and have to learn to ground ourselves, we can feel energy flying around the body, it can make us feel utterly exhausted, extremely joyful and much more besides. The fatigue was quite alarming in the beginning and I recall going to my doctor and asking what could be the cause of this unbelievable exhaustion, and he could find nothing wrong with me. I remember one particular morning having taken my three children to school; I did my meditation, fell asleep and woke up in horror at 3 o'clock in the afternoon just in time to pick the children up again. I had been asleep all day!

During my training to be a yoga teacher, I recall one of the assistants helping on the course saying that he was appalled that someone had begun crying during meditation and this was all wrong. I was horrified at his obvious lack of understanding. Crying is very beneficial, tears release stress and are very healing. Keeping pain and distress locked in is harmful and can cause illness.

Glastonbury

I began running my own spiritual development groups in my home and also joined a wonderful meditation group in Glastonbury, Somerset, in South West England, where many ley lines meet and where the ancient Abbey, the Tor, the Chalice Well and surrounding areas all contribute to make this place magical and fascinating. It is a place of very strong mixed energies with at least 59 religions registered there. I attended the meditation class there weekly for 18 months and was astonished at how it affected me. For the first few months, after a session there, I would be two days with the deepest fatigue imaginable afterwards, until I got used to the energies.

I entered one shop there with a friend and half collapsed, I had to sit down with my head in my lap while the shop owner got me some water. He sternly told me that I must use my power wisely and never misuse it; at the time, I was totally confused and couldn't get out of the shop quick enough. Another bookshop I entered made me feel so ill I had to leave immediately and I found out afterwards, that somebody had been murdered upstairs. The last time I visited Glastonbury, I parked my car, got out and almost collapsed again. I had to hastily put my spiritual protection in place around myself before I could even walk down the street.

It is a strange and fascinating place. The Tor is a tower on the top of a hill where Henry VIII's men hanged the monks from the Abbey, during the dissolution of the monasteries. It is a pleasant climb to get there and some years ago, I heard about a group of monks who visited there and one of them was suddenly lifted off the ground and was hovering about 20 feet in the air, the rest of the monks had to fall on their knees and pray to bring him back down to earth.

In the late 1980s, a friend and I climbed up that hill to the Tor at 3 a.m. along with hundreds of other people, for a Harmonic Convergence and related to the dawn of the Age of Aquarius. We stumbled in the dark, climbing the hill, falling over bodies in sleeping bags everywhere and then as the dawn began, everyone gathered, along with Sir George Trevelyan and we all meditated and prayed. Later down below, began sacred dancing around the trees to welcome in this new age. It was a very beautiful and enchanting experience and if you missed it, there would be another 33,000 years to wait for the next one!

Kundalini

Despite feeling very odd at times as a result of so much spiritual practice, in the summer of 1988 I began to feel decidedly strange, much stranger than normal and so strange in fact that I felt quite frightened. Huge energy rushes were pouring around my body and into my head; I seemed unable to ground myself, and felt completely spaced out half the time and I was not able to control it. I wasn't sure what was happening although I instinctively knew that it was connected to my meditation and spiritual practices.

Looking through the fascinating bookshops in Glastonbury at that time, I came upon a book called *The Kundalini Experience* by Lee Sannella, MD, and picking it up and reading some of it, I realised that this was what was happening to me, I was having a Kundalini awakening. I was obviously led to that book as it has since then helped me so much; there were times when I wasn't sure how I would have ever coped without it. Over the years, dipping in and out of this book, it was a godsend to me. Every strange and frightening experience I was having, seemed to be discussed in this book which gave me great comfort and support. It was the only support I had. I had nobody to talk to about it, I knew nobody who was experiencing such things and I just had to have faith.

Some years ago, I wrote to Dr Sannella to thank him for his help and described some of my experiences but unfortunately, I sent it to a previous address he had, and some of it was returned to me. I have recently learned that he has passed away in 2010 aged 93.

Nowadays, one can Google 'Kundalini awakening' or 'Kundalini symptoms' and there is a whole shaft of information available. But from what I have now seen on the web, there are a great many people suffering and not understanding what is happening to them. There is intense fear in some cases and utter despair, and standard medical doctors do not understand what it is all about. I also see that most people writing about their experiences seem to be having so many negative experiences.

Fortunately, in that autumn, just a few weeks ahead, I had booked into a 5-day Kundalini course with Lilla Bek, an NFSH healer and teacher, and she confirmed that yes, I did indeed have a Kundalini awakening and the course proved to be very interesting.

That was a long time ago as I write and with the experiences I have had, and with these energies still affecting me, I feel that I have become very well acquainted with Kundalini and its effects. As I write, it has been 26 years since Kundalini energy started to affect me, and still, I have periods where it is flooding my body and other times when I am free of it. There is very little understanding about it here in the west. When Kundalini begins to unleash, we are not able to stop it and it will continue affecting our lives, bodies, minds and souls. I personally do not agree with deliberately trying to force Kundalini to unleash in our bodies, as some classes try to do, because we do not have enough understanding of how it affects us.

It seems that there are many people who have this Kundalini energy going on in their bodies due to the increased and widespread meditation practices taking place, but do not have the spiritual understanding to go with it. My personal experience has been extensive and very varied. I understand that once this Kundalini force starts, our lives can change dramatically; they can fall apart and be rebuilt.

For myself, not long after my Kundalini awakening, we moved our family to Spain, my 26-year marriage collapsed and my life could not have been more painful or more different. My whole family ended up in different countries and it felt like the end of the world to me. I cannot be sure if the unleashing of this powerful energy contributed anything to do with how my life changed. My life in Spain, together with all its dramas and a great many cases of healings, has been documented in my book *Calamares and Corruption*.

I know that our lives can fall apart if we are meant to be fulfilling our soul's path and we can have some very strong lessons which enable us to progress spiritually. Trying to see this or understand it whilst we are in the throes of what seems like a major disaster zone, can be frankly impossible. In the midst of a major crisis, it is pretty difficult to work out what on earth is going on, as we are too busy trying to survive. Looking back now, I know I had to move to Spain to help sort out a very corrupt mayor and his gang of thieving associates.

Early 'symptoms' of Kundalini are many, including waves of energy and heat in all areas of the body, pain in various parts of the body, tingling, itching and feeling completely spaced out. As mine progressed over time, I had a huge variety of different experiences. I had periods of intense sexual desire which was so strong, it was frankly terrifying. I felt attracted to someone in my village and when I looked at him across a square or a room, I would have explosions of light bursting in my head like some kind of spiritual orgasm.

Many times, I have felt that I was losing my mind. I have had a lot of pain and discomfort in various centres of my body where blockages are being removed. For about 12 months, I had pain in the anus and womb areas and got checked out with my doctor. Mysterious bodily symptoms have suddenly appeared to make me think I was ill and have disappeared just as quickly. Indigestion and food intolerance has been rampant at times due to the body becoming more and more sensitive from the purification. The fatigue, at times, has been so severe to cause me to think I was dying.

At times, in the midst of particularly difficult times with these energies, I have had a very strong impulse to be near water and have learned that sitting by a river, lake or stream or the sea can greatly help to calm down this energy and normalise and balance it. A salt bath can also be helpful. Fill the bath with hot water, just hot enough to be comfortable and dissolve three or four tablespoons of sea salt, then soak in this for 30–40 minutes. This detoxes and helps to calm down the Kundalini energy.

Of course, there are tremendous benefits to be gained by this spiritual power, once we can get through all the difficulties. It is a process of superior cleansing and healing, far more powerful than anything we can muster up ourselves, and far superior to any therapy we can think of. This is the therapy of all therapies, a powerful spiritual process with blessings beyond our wildest imagination. Once we can establish that in fact, we do have this Kundalini rampantly operating in our systems, then the main quality we need is faith. We simply need to hand over to God or the Infinite Power, knowing that all is well and we have nothing to fear. Unfortunately, fear and even terror is very common and perfectly understandable when we struggle to understand what on earth is going on, especially in the beginning.

The benefits of this Kundalini energy coursing through our bodies is to purify and sensitize us and therefore, open up our other senses, clear and open our chakras, the spiritual centres of our bodies and offload all our negative beliefs and conditioning. In this way, we soar upwards to the heavens towards a heavenly state of being where we can see other realms of existence, we become more and more into a state of joy and peace and our lives change out of all recognition in that we leave behind all states of fear, worry and anxiety. We virtually move into another state where we laugh so much more, and we enjoy and appreciate everything in a different way. In fact, we move out of the third earthly dimension into the fourth and fifth dimensions.

Amidst the difficult symptoms I was experiencing in the beginning, I began to see massive white light in my head, even though it was dark and my eyes were closed. I experienced light exploding in my head during the day, began to see angels, nature spirits and hear the spirit world speaking to me much more clearly.

A Wonderful Experience

Something extraordinary happened several years ago and is still continuing, one night while I was wide awake and in the pitch dark, suddenly my room became filled with this wonderful pale golden light, at first I thought it must be a car's headlights and I looked out the window and saw nothing but black. The light became stronger and stronger and the entire room was radiating the most beautiful golden glow, I was simply mesmerised and must also confess that I was quite frightened.

As I lay there, the golden colour slowly changed to purple and all over the walls there appeared huge circles of swirling light; they looked like giant Catherine wheels. There were dozens of them and they spun around whilst over the ceiling and other walls, swirling and pulsating light and colours continued to blaze. I watched all this in amazement and after a few minutes, it all started to subside and gradually faded away. I was left wondering what on earth it had been about. After it had all stopped, I wished it would all come back but I felt quite unnerved by it all.

I didn't have to wait long, within a few days, the same thing happened and continued every few days until I eventually had to discuss it with my husband (with whom I was now reconciled) as I was feeling overwhelmed by it and a bit frightened. Considering he used to be very sceptical about all these things, he was very supportive and told me to relax, not be afraid and just enjoy the lights. This has now been going on for years, each time it takes a different form, but the colours are usually gold and purple. They often pulsate very strongly.

As we progress spiritually, we begin to see 'dead' people and realise that they are not dead at all but living somewhere else; we start to see angels, elementals and fairies around plants and trees, and different dimensions and worlds which exist outside our own. Many people long to have their inner vision opened and their third eye functioning, and have a great desire to see the spirit world. These abilities are usually brought about by a lot of dedication, and it can be a slow process with which we need a lot of patience. Some people are, of course, natural psychics from childhood. However, visions such as these can be brought about by meditation and also by the awakening of Kundalini energy which I strongly believe should never be deliberately forced.

I now realise that my own experiences with Kundalini energy have been greatly helped by – first, the only book I have on the subject which has been heaven-sent and without which I would never have coped – and secondly, and perhaps most importantly, by my prayers, my belief that this was a spiritual happening and I needed to accept it because it was worthwhile. My constant prayers for help have indeed eased the symptoms and constantly guided me to understand what is going on. Also, my dreams have answered some of the problems.

On the Other Side

Many years ago, meditating alone at home, I saw a spirit come towards me across the room, go over my head and I was transported into the next world. I saw what was like a pyramid rising up towards a very vivid light, and as I looked up, I saw on each side saints and angels. I was slowly travelling upwards by the side of this pyramid, towards the light, and I looked down and saw a very dark bottomless region and thought I was glad I wasn't down there.

I then started to ask questions, I said, "But where are the healing rooms?" I was instantly transported to rows of utterly beautiful small rooms, all in the most heavenly pastel colours I have ever seen, in pale green, pale pink, pale blue and delicate gold. In each room, there was a bed with someone lying on it and, beside them, someone administering assistance. I then said, "But where are the gardens?" Next, I was surrounded by wonderful gardens full of lovely flowers and trees. I asked where the animals were and I was shown animals of every description, living and grazing peacefully. I then asked where my parents were and they appeared in front of me very close, and at that moment, I was brought back to my sitting room. I was then told that they had brought me back at that point so that I would not get upset.

Over the years, I have run many spiritual development groups both in Spain and South West England. The purpose of a development group is to increase spiritual awareness which, at the same time, helps to heal our bodies and minds and also guide us. Our third eye on the forehead can be opened so that we can see other worlds.

None of us can know for certainty how it all functions on the other side because although we have been there many times, after passing over from past lives, those memories are removed from us as we are born again. However, during our group meetings, we have had many insights which I go into later in the book.

House Cleansings and Sending Spirits Over

In our home in Somerset, when the children were young, all sorts of strange happenings and activities began to take place. We heard odd noises that we were unable to identify, articles disappeared and reappeared in different places. We were all accusing each other of hiding things. Gradually, these activities increased in intensity and it all became very curious. Everybody swore they hadn't moved the things that were vanishing.

One incident was when I couldn't find my coat, I searched the house up and down and nobody had seen it. I had last worn it a few days before whilst shopping, and I rang the police and the various shops I had been in to see if it had been found. It was my favourite coat, and I was pretty upset about it. About two weeks later, when one of my daughter's friends came to stay overnight, I went into one of our walk-in lofts upstairs to look for bedding, and there on the floor was my coat. I called the children and showed them, and we were all quite amazed. The poor girl, who was staying the night, became quite terrified as she had heard about all the strange goings-on in our house! She wanted to go home, but we managed to calm her down.

Around this time, I was becoming very aware of colours and I had a small bouquet of yellow silk flowers in a vase; I cut off a small branch and decided to keep it on my person as I felt I needed this colour at that time. At night, I would place these small yellow flowers next to my bed on the bedside table. This went on for some weeks, and then one morning when I woke up, these flowers had turned blue. I cannot describe my amazement; I called my children and pointed it out to my husband, who was very sceptical about all these things, and they all agreed that they knew it had been yellow, but, of course, even though the evidence is before your eyes, it can be very hard to take in. Obviously, I must have needed the colour blue and spirit had brought it forth, but, nevertheless, it was quite an extraordinary happening.

There was another strange occurrence when I was cooking and needed a tin of red kidney beans. I had gone through my larder containing various tinned foods, and I did not have one. I was rather disappointed and checked again, I did not have many tins and, no, there were no beans, and so I left it. Later in the day, I had reason to get something else out of my larder and there, right in the front of the tins, was a tin of kidney beans. My children, who were disbelieving everything, as it was all so weird and wonderful, told me that it had obviously been there all the time and I must have not seen it. However, I know that that tin had appeared quite magically, despite everybody's disbelief.

Our House Guest

As time went on, we heard tapping on the internal doors and also on our front door, but there was never anybody there. One night, our son, who was 14 at the time, agreed to take care of the younger children whilst we went out to dinner, but there was such loud tapping on the sitting room door from the kitchen that he was driven to bed at 7 p.m. with his head under the duvet.

At that time, I had no experience of stuck souls and I had no idea what was going on. After a group meditation in my house, I mentioned it to a friend, and she said, "Oh I thought you knew, there is a lady here, I've seen her walking up and down the stairs whilst we were meditating." I was pretty astonished as I hadn't seen her at that time. Matters got more intense; I would wake up in the night as there would be crashing going on downstairs and I would go down to investigate, thinking we had a burglar, and would find nothing.

Then I would hear heavy footsteps coming up the stairs, and one night, someone breathed heavily in my face. Our boxer dog would often suddenly stand up and growl at something across the room that we couldn't see. Every day, as my daughter was coming home from school, walking down the lane from getting off the school bus, she would see this small lady, all in brown, waiting on the step outside the gate, but as she got closer, the lady would disappear.

Then on the evening of Christmas Day, I was in the kitchen and I looked up and saw a small person all in brown, walking towards me, but I could see straight through her. I was shaken and called my husband and refused to go back into the kitchen that evening. Now I realised that we really did have a soul or 'ghost' as some people will say walking about the house. Of course, I realise now that the poor soul was trying to attract my

120

attention but at the time, it was pretty frightening and I knew nothing about sending souls on.

The last straw was when I was alone meditating in my sitting room, I heard a dreadful loud wail which went on and on and I got a very big fright. Fortunately, my husband had just pulled up outside and got out of his car and also heard it. We both ran about outside the house and could not find anybody; our house was remote in the countryside. We searched the inside of the house also. By this time, my knees were shaking uncontrollably and I had to drive off to see a friend for a couple of hours.

I realised that this had been the spirit calling to me and I finally knew that she needed help and I prayed for help myself to deal with it. Whilst meditating, I asked for this soul to come close and speak to me. It was a very sad tale. She was very young about 21 years old; she had lived during the 1500s in a hut which was on our land before the house was built. She lived with her parents and they were very poor. She told me that she had rejected the advances of a young man who wanted to court her and he then went and drowned himself in a pond. Then later, her parents died and she starved to death. As a result of all her suffering, she had not been able to pass over into the light.

That evening, I asked my children to sit with me on the floor, we sat in a circle and we all prayed for her together. I asked God and the angels to surround this person with love and light and asked that she be taken to the spirit world where she could rest in peace. I asked that she would be with her family and loving souls. I then saw a movement and felt her leaving. We thanked God for helping her and us. All the strange activities relating to her ceased and a few weeks later, she came back and thanked us for helping her.

The Organist

All sorts of strange things continued in our house when we moved to a tiny mountain village in Spain where we lived for many years. One night, one of my daughters was calling out to me and I went in to find her bed had been moved half way across the room while she was asleep. Then one evening, I had a 'visit' from a gentleman in the spirit world who told me that he had been the church organist there. Despite this being a tiny village, it had a simply huge and beautiful church with a magnificent organ and our house was just behind this church. He told me the sad tale that he had played the organ there for many years and nobody had ever thanked him or made any comment to him whatsoever about his playing. He said he couldn't pass over because he was so upset and felt extremely unappreciated.

As I am a pianist, and also took guitar lessons for a couple of years, I could certainly understand how he felt. Whenever I hear live music, I always make a point of thanking and congratulating the musicians afterwards. All my children had piano and flute lessons for many years, and my daughters still play and my son plays the drums. I recall I was the only person who thanked and congratulated the lovely harpist at my daughter's wedding and took an interest in the instrument and how she played it. She mentioned this to my daughter afterwards, and said how pleased she had been with the interest I took.

On this occasion, I was wondering what to do about this gentleman as I did not relish the thought of going around the village and getting the people to apologise to this man, and thank him, as you can imagine, that was unthinkable. So I decided that I would have to thank him myself on behalf of the people of the village. I talked with him and told him that I understood the need to be appreciated, I said I knew about playing the piano as I had been playing since I was six years old. I still own and play the piano, which belonged to my mother who had played all her life. I had taken it to Spain (and many years later brought it back to England).

I was one of four children, and only my brother and I continued playing the piano all our lives, my two sisters did not. I felt it was only fair to my mother to continue playing, after she had walked me a couple of miles to piano lessons every week for eight years. I told the organist that my brother and brother-in-law had both played the organ in our local churches at home and both were simply brilliant pianists. My brother-in-law owned a Bechstein piano and loved playing the classics and my brother owned a grand piano and had his own jazz band for many years. He also played in the top nightclubs in London, where he too was ignored and never complimented. His daughters also play very well. I remember wonderful times as a child with big family parties when both my brother and brother-in-law were playing the piano together, one at each end, with lots of singing going on.

I then apologised to him on behalf of the people of the village that they had not ever thanked him, and told him that even though I hadn't known him, I most certainly did appreciate all he had done for the church. I told him that I realised playing the organ was a great skill and it was very noble of him to have done so for many years. He seemed very heartened by all I told him. At the end of this conversation, I prayed to Jesus and the angels and asked that they come and escort this man to the light and I saw this happening. About two months later, he returned and thanked me for what I had done and said he was very grateful for my help.

An Amusing Incident

This happened when my daughter and I went to a party which was in a house in the Andalucían hills, seemingly in the middle of nowhere, which we had difficulty in finding, a large finca with a lot of land and so we arrived a bit late. It was a party for about 40 healers and mediums and as we walked in, there were about eight people standing around a table with their hands touching the top edges. Someone called out to me and said, "Hurry and put your hands on this table."

Not sure what was going on, I did as I was told and they moved up and made room for me. I lightly touched the edge of the table with my fingertips as the others were doing and immediately the table just lifted off and flew several feet up vertically in the air and went sideways across the room. I fell over and landed on top of someone and I must confess I got the most uncontrollable bout of giggling; it was such an extraordinary sight

My daughter was only about 11 years old and had been stood behind me. I did think this might well have frightened her but as children do, she didn't believe that it had spontaneously happened, she thought someone had pushed it into the air. I was then told off by the hostess for laughing so much, as she said it had been a serious experiment! Some of the healing work I did in Spain is documented in my book *Calamares and Corruption,* and in a further book which I am also writing.

Sending Souls On

Over the years, I have been called out to dozens of homes to clear unwanted and stuck souls who are disturbing people. There have been many interesting cases. One lady called me in and said a lady's hat regularly fell off the top of the wardrobe, and she also frequently saw her son who had passed over. She asked me to check out the bedroom and see what was going on there but asked me not to send her son away, as she had great comfort from his visits. Naturally, I honoured this request.

Her son had died three years previously; he had hanged himself in a tree in hospital grounds. He quickly approached me and said he was very sorry for what he had done and to cause his mother so much suffering. He had been in south East Asia and had come back early. His mother said that the malaria tablets had caused him to change, but he told me that he had dabbled in drugs and I also picked up some black magic involvement. Usually, suicide cases do not pass into the light but he had, due no doubt to his mother's prayers.

We do need to pray for our deceased loved ones that they may pass into the light. I recall my own brother-in-law, who died suddenly in his fifties, who had no spiritual understanding or belief and after he passed over, I would see him floating about not knowing where he was. I prayed for him over a period of about two weeks and he passed over into the light. He has returned and asked for a message to be given to his partner, but she also does not believe and was not interested.

I went upstairs to find out why the hat kept jumping off the wardrobe. There I saw a tiny little lady, hunched over, with wispy hair. She desperately needed help and said she was so grateful that I was trying to help her. She told me she had been very lonely and had died a terrible long drawn out death. She had been a spinster with no family, apart from one relative who lived next door and who only visited once a week, standing on the doorstep. Nobody bothered with her, they ignored her and she felt thoroughly neglected. I listened to her and talked to her and gave her compassion and love and prayed for her to pass over into the light and be met by loved ones there.

Another situation was where a lady was seeing various people wandering about her home and was very disturbed by it all. She was also being touched on her legs and feet and pushed about. Although the house was about 20 years old, there were spirits there from a previous dwelling. I ascertained that there had been bitter rivalry more than 100 years ago between two men over a lady, I saw a man with curly hair and he said he had lost out and the lady had married a man I could see in a top hat. He then shot this man and then shot himself. I also was able to detect that two children had died in the area at childbirth, so there was a great deal of suffering about. I cleared the house of all lower energies and prayed that all spirits be surrounded by light and love and sent to their appointed place in the next world. I then asked for the whole house to be filled with light and love.

In some homes, I am simply asked to cleanse the house, with no spirits involved. This includes going from room to room and outside gardens also, clearing negativity and sending it down into the ground to be transmuted into light. I have seen piles of grey matter pouring from the walls, like dust, but that is thought forms and negative emotions that build up and stay caught in the house in its very fabric. People who have lived in the house can leave behind some of their pain, anguish and illness, leaving sad and lonely vibrations. Where children have been cruelly treated or physical harm committed, intense fear and anger can be left behind. Violent arguments will leave harmful and negative vibrations.

If there has been illness or grief in the house, it is a good idea to have it cleansed in this way. Otherwise, have days where all the windows are wide open to bring in fresh air to circulate, and this will help. You can also have bowls of crystals in your main rooms which have been blessed and energised, and these will help to clear lower vibrations. These crystals need to be washed regularly and left in water with some sea salt soaking for a couple of hours.

126

A Poor Mouse

An interesting case was in a post office where the owners were quite psychic and very often saw something moving about their property but couldn't quite make out what it was. They felt it was an animal of some kind. First, I felt a deep black negative energy in the sitting room, I saw a grey haired gentleman who had died there about 100 years previously; he had died in pain, misery and poverty and although his soul was not stuck there, he had left all the negative energy behind. I cleared all this energy and filled the house with light.

Then I clearly saw a very large mouse, he had been stuck there for a very long time, because he had been caught in a mousetrap for 3–4 days in excruciating pain before he died. He was very cross indeed and told me to tell everyone to never use traps, as they are extremely cruel and cause horrific suffering. He said to use a humane trap and carry the live animal out into the fields and let it free. I told him that I was deeply sorry for what had happened to him, surrounded him with light and love and sent him into the light. As he was leaving, he called out, "Animals have souls."

The owners of the house confirmed that this must have happened before they had moved in ten years previously, as they knew nothing about it. She is an animal lover and her own cat visits her regularly from the spirit world, he had lived until he was 27 and when he comes, he takes out her hair grips which is what he used to do when he was alive.

Unfortunately, I made the mistake of telling a neighbour of mine, with whom I was quite friendly about the mouse as I thought she may find it interesting, but she was aghast and was extremely rude to me. This was a valuable lesson to me as I realised that it is never worth discussing precious experiences with people who have critical closed minds and no understanding or knowledge about such matters. Since then, I have never shared such experiences with anyone.

This is the same person whose mother from the spirit world was stood next to her on many occasions begging me to give her a message. I hesitated as I felt she would not believe me and when finally I told her that her mother wished to speak to her, she went quite berserk and was again extremely rude.

On another occasion, because this lady was a very recent convert to Christianity, she was a born again Christian, I foolishly shared with her my vision of Jesus Christ thinking it would inspire her. Instead, she was horrified and told me that Jesus would never come to a person 'like you'. Knowing that this friendship could not continue as I was not prepared to be insulted or ridiculed by anyone; I was greatly relieved when shortly afterwards, this lady moved away. I no longer discuss any such matters with anyone apart from my spiritual friends.

A Huge Job

I had a massive job in a village which lasted for about 12 months. When I returned to England after living for several years in Spain, I rented a cottage and was working all hours, as I had four cats and my boxer dog in quarantine kennels for six months, which was costing a great deal of money. Our horse was in stables. As well as doing my healing work with private consultations, I was doing a lot of nursing shifts in private houses, nursing homes and hospitals.

One house where I worked turned out to be an extraordinary job in so many different ways. I was taking care of a gentleman in a wheelchair with breathing problems, and working some day-shifts there but mostly night shifts. The house was a very large and beautiful Victorian mansion, with a wonderful sweeping spiral staircase, very high ceilings, all painted in stunning colours. The room in which I slept was painted a dark turquoise on the walls with a dark green ceiling. All the floors in the house had wide oak floorboards; all stained a dark brown. I worked for these people for some years and we became good friends.

They were both in need of healing and asked that during my shifts, could I give them both a healing each time I was there, which I was happy to do. After I had been working there for a while, the gentleman's wife, Betty, told me that her husband, John, was possessed by his father. Now I had never come across a possession and at that time found it very hard to believe. Betty is psychic and could see and sense all sorts of things but wasn't able to deal with them. She asked me if I could remove this possession from her husband.

Evidently, John's father had dominated and controlled him throughout his life and was still trying to do so, after he had passed over. She told me that he had been a very unpleasant man. Betty attended her local church regularly and asked the vicar if he could help with this problem, but he was unable to and despite contacting the Church Authorities, nobody seemed able to do anything or support them in any way. The local vicar came and sprinkled holy water around the house but this did not help.

Betty wanted me to shout at this possession, at her father-in-law, and tell him to leave immediately, as she felt this would be the only way to deal with it. I certainly did not agree and told her that love would sort the problem out. She was appalled that I should want to send love to someone who she saw as evil. I began to send love to John and his father. Love, after all, is the highest power of all. I prayed and asked Jesus Christ for his help. I asked for help from angels, Archangels and the highest source of light. For the first two or three sessions, I didn't see any sign of possession and was still very uncertain that Betty was right. During the next healing, I saw a large black shape almost filling his body which slipped out and slithered away across the floor and appeared to disappear beneath the floorboards. I felt that this then had solved the problem and we were all very hopeful.

However, a few days later Betty rang me to inform me that he was back, dwelling in her husband again, she knew because she could see it and also her husband was badly affected. She once again asked me to shout at this spirit and tell him to leave them alone and go away. I realised that I was really up against something here. It has been my experience that love will usually solve most problems, and I was determined to do it my way. I felt that for whatever reason this soul was occupying his son's body; he needed help and healing too.

For the next session, I protected us all before I began with very powerful protection, and then embarked on more healing asking that light and love be poured into John, I saw white and gold light pouring in, and emerald green light filling up his whole being. I held on to these prayers and continued pouring in light and love. I prayed strongly that this soul would be moved away and sent into the light. Then finally, this was achieved, and the soul was released from his son's body and taken to the light. Fortunately, he never came back and everybody was very relieved, myself included.

5th Century Battle

That event was only the beginning of the extraordinary events which took place in this house. Not long after this, Betty began to see two or three spirits at the end of her bed during the night. As you can imagine, she found this very disturbing. Again, she contacted the church as she felt very strongly that they should be able to help but once again, apart from some holy water being sprinkled about, no help was forthcoming. She even went so far as to go to meetings with a group of people purporting to be the psychic and research sector of the church, but she felt very strongly that they thought she was making the whole thing up and did nothing whatsoever to help her.

I was extremely busy with a lot of other work so was not able to be with her more than a couple of times a week. She rang and asked me to go over again to see what on earth was going on. I linked into these souls and they explained that they had died in a brutal battle. What we did not expect was that this was to continue for about a year with spirits appearing every night. Betty was at her wits end with it all, I was fortunate not to be living there and able to escape to my peaceful cottage.

Thankfully, Betty had a friend who is a retired church vicar; he is a healer and psychic medium but he had to keep quiet about his abilities whilst working for the church due to their disapproval. He lived quite a long way away but when he could, he also began to help with this situation, which was very welcome as it was overwhelming. Every night, Betty was being visited by spirits who were stuck and needed help to pass over.

I decided to go outside in their beautiful gardens and tune in to see what was going on. There I saw a horrible battle across the fields with raggedy people running about armed with alarming weapons chopping heads off. I was told that this was a battle from the 5th century and was so violent that the people involved were stuck in between worlds. As we began to send them on one or two at a time, it seemed never ending, for as soon as we helped them more would arrive.

What was happening was that these spirits were being attracted to the people who could help them. What we didn't realise in the beginning was that there were more than 200 of them. When it was all over after a long period of time dealing with all these souls, I ended up walking around the fields behind their home and around their village clearing the whole land and area. Where battles and murders have taken place; these areas need healing, for negative vibrations are left behind. The way to do this is to call on God for help, the highest light, the highest souls of love and healing, and ask and then see the area being filled with white light. I then see any negativity or pain that has been left behind, going down into the earth to be transmuted into white light. The earth has the ability to transmute negativity.

One day in the middle of all this, Betty heard some commotion in her cellar but waited for both me and her vicar friend to be present together, and asked us to go down into the cellar to investigate. I have to say I was rather filled with trepidation. It is a simply enormous cellar, the size of the whole house, divided into many beautiful rooms with archways between, the floors laid in wonderful cobbles, but nevertheless dark and creepy, cold, dank and clammy.

Betty armed her friend and me with a torch each and we set off gingerly down the steep stone steps whilst Betty stayed at the top peering down. The vicar went first and before he had reached the bottom step he began shouting loudly and waving his arms. I think it is from this wonderful gentleman that Betty had learnt that one should shout at spirits. I stood rooted to the step with my back up against the wall quite unnerved. He then proceeded into the cellar rooms still wildly shouting and gesticulating.

Still glued to the spot half way down the cellar, I suddenly saw a row of dead bodies in some kind of uniform, covered in many wounds and bandages laid out in a row on the floor.

There were about 10 men laid there and I guessed the cellar had been used at some time to lay wounded or dead soldiers until they could be buried or treated. Whilst our friend was going around the cellar shouting at I don't know who, I got on and prayed for these poor souls who were still stuck, surrounding them with light and love and asking that they be taken into the light. They too had needed help to pass over. I then proceeded to explore the cellar rooms with the vicar but I personally saw nothing else.

We joined Betty for a very welcome cup of tea in the warm kitchen and since then, she and I have often laughed about this event, as she had been quite terrified stood at the top of the steps. Even though it is a serious and moving affair to send souls on, we do have to keep our sense of humour.

This whole business of helping souls to pass into the light is very important. 'Ghosts' or wandering spirits do not want to be stuck, they need help. They remain stuck for many different reasons. Sometimes the soul cannot move away from their home, it could have been intensely important to them and they just cannot leave it behind. It can be that they cannot leave their money and material possessions. Sometimes, it is because there has been a lot of family upsets and they were not resolved.

They can remain stuck because they were involved in deep trauma, such as war, or deep unhappiness for various reasons. A spirit cannot go into the light or have peace if their loved ones on earth cannot let them go. A medium needs to 'tune in' or link with a spirit and let them explain how they feel, what has happened. Appropriate comfort needs to be given and then the process of helping them pass over takes place.

It is necessary to remember, of course, that this is all done with the help of our guides and angels; I always call on Jesus to help in such cases, but always that help has to come from the highest form of light and love. Furthermore, we are channels of this light and always have to protect ourselves before beginning anything of this nature, and this too is prayed for; a simple prayer asking for complete protection. Archangel Michael will help with protection. I call on him and I also protect myself with three layers of gold light, like an egg completely surrounding my body, then three layers of silver light and finally three layers of purple light, and I am cocooned within these lights. Always after procedures such as these, I ask Archangel Michael to clear me, my aura and the whole of me, and take down into the earth any negativity I may have picked up, to be transmuted into white light.

We can call on Archangel Michael and ask him to protect our families and us every day, and also protect our homes, vehicles and journeys. Angels are more than willing to help us but we need to ask. We may see small white feathers and not know where they have come from and this can be an indication that angels are around us. When I was giving healing to Tammy, our horse, I had a small white feather fall from my sitting room ceiling into my lap, two more were stuck to my mobile phone. I would find them in my handbag and one day after thoroughly hoovering the floor, I found one on the carpet. One day I had one stuck to my little finger. They comforted me considerably and gave me strength to continue believing she could be healed.

Nature Spirits

As we progress and our third eye opens, we begin to see other realms of life and existence. There is a great deal of interest now in spiritual matters and therefore, I will talk about nature spirits, although after beginning to see them, I told nobody for many years. My grown up children, although open to healing, are quite sceptical about psychic occurrences, despite all the activity in our home when they were growing up.

I began by sending love to trees, plants and shrubs whilst out walking or sitting in the garden. I had by then been sending love and talking to trees for many years. When I was walking our horses out, I would tell the trees and plants that they were beautiful and often saw sparkling light around them. Curiously, a client of mine had insisted that I surely could speak to animals and as soon as I tried, I found I could communicate very well. This proved to be very useful when giving healing to animals.

One day whilst out walking with a friend in a forest, I suddenly saw a beautiful large mauve butterfly flitting from one bush to another a few feet away. I pointed it out to my friend but she couldn't see it. I got very excited and said, "Look there on that bush," where it sat very clearly. Still she couldn't see it. It then disappeared. I walked to the bush and searched for it, and was quite amazed that it was no longer there. It then dawned on me that it was a nature spirit. It was February, very cold, the trees were mostly bare and I realised that we don't have large mauve butterflies in England, as far as I knew, especially not in the middle of winter. It was my first encounter with a nature spirit and I was very excited. Since then I have seen many more outside and indoors. Often when I am buying plants, one will call out to me to buy it.

Since then during healings, I have seen fairies all over various clients' bodies. It appears they have strong powers of their own. I see gnomes sometimes with me when I am working. I struggled at first to believe what I was seeing, but gradually came to accept them. For those having a hard time to believe that elementals and nature spirits exist, I have written more about this later in the book.

I had an interesting encounter in Switzerland whilst staying with a friend of mine many years ago, when she took me to a Butterfly Sanctuary. As we walked into the heated butterfly space, I became covered utterly with exotic butterflies landing on me. I had two huge butterflies on my forehead, they seemed to be massaging my skin; all sorts of species were on my head, all over me. People stared in amusement and I was quite confused as to why on earth I was covered and nobody else was. I had to stand there for some time, as I didn't like to disturb them. They didn't leave me so I had to start walking very slowly around the sanctuary and it wasn't until I was leaving that they finally flew away.

The result of that encounter was that I couldn't sleep a single wink when I went to bed that night, I was quite totally awake and wondering what on earth was going on. We had to abandon the next day's plans as I was too tired to go. It is thought that butterflies are angels of some sort, and once again, I realised that nature spirits have a power of their own and no doubt, they were working on me in some way…

One time during meditation, I asked Pan who is at a very high spiritual level, various questions and then asked about the two books I am writing and asked for his advice. We were surrounded by angels; creatures with wings about 4–5 feet high. I had my first completed manuscript about Spain in my hands, and these winged creatures then took it, threw the manuscript from one to the other, energizing it. Then a huge strange looking bird – which may have been a phoenix – took it in his beak and flew up into the intense sun-like light and then returned a short while later, and said it had been blessed by God. I then said, "What about the healing book I am at present writing," the one you are now reading, and I saw it having the same treatment, angels throwing it between them and then the bird taking it up into the light and having it blessed. At that moment, I had no doubt that both these books would be published.

We chose to meditate on flowers one evening in our development group, and I was astonished at the power I felt from them; we went for a walk in meditation and I had daffodils calling out to me. Then I saw tiny mauve violets in a wood, which were my mother's favourite flower, but was drawn into a garden to a huge dark red peony which is one of my favourite flowers and was taken right inside it. Fairies were running up and down the stem and all over; they said they are desperate to speak to me, and will I go outside to listen. They said the peony was like my life, very rich and full – children, family, animals, horses, work and lots going on. I said I am very grateful.

I then went outside on a mild day that week, sat on a chair and asked the fairies what they wanted to tell me. They told me to concentrate on my desires, to read and think about them night and morning, and to give thanks for their manifestation and not to give up.

As for flowers, it seems that they all have an extraordinary power, I felt it and each flower has meaning, power and messages to give us. I found this utterly amazing. Of course, Dr Edward Bach was led to feel certain emotions and was then led to discover the appropriate plant to use to heal those emotions. He then created the Bach flower remedies to heal all sorts of ailments.

I have always been very affected by flowers, especially irises and can understand how they can bring up strong emotions. I have a watercolour of an iris which someone had painted for me and I felt such strong emotions about leaving the irises my father bought for me when I moved house. I always regretted not taking them with me but this is partly due I think to the fact that they were a present from my father. It is extraordinary how powerfully they can affect us. I have noticed this time and time again, when I have seen plants I used to own and no longer do. So fresh flowers both outside and in the house are obviously very important.

Passing on Messages from the Spirit World

As healers and mediums, we have a responsibility to help others and I have often been asked to give messages from the spirit world to people but this can be very tricky as a lot of people simply do not believe that the soul lives on after death.

I describe a case here where a family I knew very well lost a teenager in an accident, and naturally, the family were distraught. At this time, my daughter and I had our horses stabled on their premises for some years and so therefore, we saw this young man growing up and were very fond of him. We had both seen him almost every day coming home from school when one of us was feeding our horses and we were deeply upset at his passing so young. However, afterwards I often saw David at the stables; he came to me so many times, asking me to speak to his parents. I tried to tell his mother but she really didn't believe. I asked her to tell her husband but she refused saying that her husband most certainly would not understand.

It states quite clearly in the Bible in Corinthians 1 chapter 12, that some will be given the gifts of healing, some the gifts of discerning of spirits, some the workings of miracles and some the gifts of prophecy and so on. Also, Jesus said, "What I can do, you can do and more." However, it is still extremely difficult for some people to accept that the soul lives on.

It is not always easy for those on the other side to make contact with people on earth, but David had been making very strong contact with me ever since he had departed. Furthermore, about six other mediums had contacted me at my church over a period of a few months with messages from this young man. The young man was very concerned that his father was keeping his grief locked in and was suffering a great deal.

He simply could not accept that he had lost his son and he was no longer there with him. The loss of a child is the worst possible thing anyone can experience and my heart went out to this family.

I was acutely aware of the pain and devastation they were all going through and my daughter and I felt this too, being so close at the time. I know that even if they could accept that David is 'living' somewhere else, it is not the same as having him sat at the table. It is not the same but it is some comfort to know that they are close by. We do not 'die', we simply go elsewhere.

One day, I arrived at the stables around my usual time in the afternoon and as I drove up, I saw the double gates to the front yard were both wide open to the road and there were two horses in the yard. I was horrified and leapt out of the car and rushed into the yard to shut the gates, hardly believing that the horses hadn't galloped off down the road. As I closed the gates in relief, I turned around and saw David standing there and he spoke to me and told me that he had been stopping them from running out until I got there. He must have been there since early morning when the family had left.

I told his mother but again she didn't believe it and would not tell her husband, she said he would say it was rubbish. After a lot of desperate messages from their son, I decided to write a letter to his father, as I was nervous to deal with him directly and also by that time our horses had been moved away to other stables. I explained all that had happened and all that had been said and gave him various messages from his son. I had done my duty and used the gift God gave me, and the rest was up to them. I made some suggestions and gave them some details of people who could help them, should they wish.

David came to me and said that he had not realised that I could do this work and therefore, had not appreciated me enough. He told me he wished he had appreciated me more. He was a lovely young man.

At the very worst of all the grief after it had happened and I was also deeply upset, I asked my spirit guides and angels why he had to die so young, I wanted to know. I was told that it had to be, that it was karmic, that they had to go through it because of something that had happened in a past life. I was not given the precise details; I was told that I would not be shown. It was a matter working out within the family. The word karmic relates to the Laws of Karma and therefore, something has happened to cause this to come about. Nothing happens by chance.

Life can be very hard indeed sometimes. We are born on earth and have to learn lessons; these are mainly love, compassion and forgiveness, and respect for all living things including animals, birds, fish and plants. We are not here just to acquire material possessions. After all, we take nothing with us when we pass over but our spiritual qualities. When our time is over, we pass to the next world where we then have many lessons to learn and eventually, when it is the right time, we are born again. We can be born anywhere and in all kinds of circumstances but we are here to learn. This is why we shouldn't judge because we live all kinds of lives. If we don't learn our lessons of love, compassion and forgiveness in this life, then we will have to learn them in the next, even going through the same scenarios, so the sooner we all learn them, the better, so we can move on to greater understandings.

Later on, I had another reason to pass on a message to bereaved parents. A couple of years ago, one of my teenage neighbours died in her sleep. I attended the funeral and the church was packed. I was sitting about six rows from the front. As we were singing a hymn, I heard a strong voice telling me to look into the far left hand corner of the church in front of me. I have to confess that I tried to ignore this voice as I find it quite difficult to pass on messages to people when I have no idea what they believe.

I was trying not to get involved, however, the voice continued and I finally looked up and saw the young girl in question. I hadn't known her very well but we had had some contact, mainly around horses and other animals. She had kindly cared for one of our horses when I went away once or twice. She informed me that I was the only one in the church who could see her. She continued to say that the circle was complete and she then turned around and walked away. What I saw was two long lines of what looked like monks in brown robes and she walked away between them.

I was then faced with wondering what to do with this information. It is different if someone comes for a reading or we are in our spiritual development group and information from spirit is expected. After a while, I decided to inform one of the family's neighbours, someone who I knew quite well. I asked him to relay the message that I had seen this girl at the church service and if the family wished to speak to me then it would be up to them. He told the girl's father but I heard no more. Some months later, I met the girl's mother and asked her if she had been informed. She hadn't so I proceeded to tell her what I had seen and heard. I presumed that 'the circle was complete' meant that she had completed her life on earth and was meant to leave. How hard this is for the poor family left behind.

Such Negative People

Sometime ago, I visited a family member who had looked at the website I had at that time which described my book about Spain, *Calamares and Corruption*, and she spent five hours criticizing me and putting me down, about living in Spain, fighting the mayor, writing the book in case I might be murdered, and many more personal insults – said she would never read the book – and within 15 minutes I was depressed and after five hours beside myself. I then spent several days very down. I tried cutting ties, shifting negative energies, lots of things, to no avail. I felt very heavy and seemed unable to shift it. I look back now and wonder why on earth I stayed for five hours to take such a diatribe of negativity, I think I was trying to be loving and kind. I know now that I should not have stayed to take such verbal abuse.

Whilst meditating later, I finally asked what on earth is going on with this family member and one other who was also being very critical. I was shown the past life where I was drowned by the church and was under the water, and a huge tie was between this person and myself and it was they who had persecuted me, condemned me and then murdered me. I was so shocked; I was quite poorly for a couple of days, utterly devoid of strength, in a state of complete exhaustion. I was told afterwards, that this was due to the negative energies involved being released from that life.

At some point, after this visit, a circle of spirits surrounded me and said they would protect me from any future attacks and it would never happen again. Spirit then told me to only visit when it is necessary and not stay too long.

A healer friend, who had moved to the coast, invited me to spend the weekend but it ended up being a revelation – my friend's husband spent the weekend ranting nonstop and condemning everything and everybody. I realised just how positive and peaceful I had become, I was so amazed to hear someone talking like that and I could hardly believe it. I had heard nobody talk like that for a very long time. I tried to get him to be more positive which seemed to pay off, as he was certainly better the next day and quite apologetic, certainly less grumpy. I suggested that he try to be grateful for what he has and to see the best in people.

However, as soon as I returned home, he evidently reverted to his normal negative state. These people have serious wealth but hold on to it tightly and search for the cheapest food, mostly out of date. They never eat out or even go out for a coffee. I often told my friend about wonderful spiritual workshops in her location but she would not spend the money. Due to the constant chronic negativity of the husband, he is forever falling over, hitting his head on branches, slipping in the ice, crashing his car and in fact, nonstop dramas surround him. This is a perfect example of how we are affected by our thoughts and words.

My friend had previously had a consultation with me, where I saw a very powerful negative energy right through her and down into the earth, like a huge black pole, grounding and stopping her, created by her extremely controlling husband. I had already seen her as a Cathar in a past life and her husband as her tormentor where the church was murdering the Cathars and they had huge thick ties to each other at the solar plexus level, which, with her cooperation I cut and burned.

The weekend amazed me – so many aspects – my own realisation of where I am, who I mix with, the lovely women and men I know and how much I have mastered my mind. Obviously, there is always much more for me to learn but I realised that I had made much headway as far as positive attitudes. These are people who have a great deal of money, a lovely spacious house and a brand new car, but it hasn't given them any peace of mind or happiness. I must add here that at this time, my life was anything but perfect. I had been separated for many years from my husband; I was living alone and was renting a flat. I was working all hours to try and get money together to attempt to buy a property.

The weekend left me feeling overwhelmed with the realisation of how peaceful and joyful, and positive I had become. The peace of mind I have worked for and obtained, I would not exchange for anything. It occurred to me that if I never had another success in my life, I had achieved a calm and loving attitude. I believe that that is success. We can achieve peace by study, meditation, listening to spirit and a lot of effort watching thoughts. I am very fortunate to have amazing support from my family, my church, my spiritual group and wonderful friends.

Gifts of spirit are states of being, rewards for hard work, qualities of peace, joy, happiness, faith, love, contentment, gratitude, generosity, kindness, these are priceless, to have wealth without these qualities is futile. We need to think joy, appreciation, gratitude, notice beauty, flowers and a beautiful world and appreciate our friends and family. After all, when we pass over into the next world, it is the spiritual qualities that we have acquired that we take with us and nothing else.

I also realised that it is extraordinary how some people later in life have learned nothing about the goodness and blessings they have, they only see everything in terms of money, that everything around them is awful, and they are full of self-pity. And, of course, the more positive we are, the more we affect the world for the better and everybody around us.

Someone I knew and liked suddenly died and it gave me quite a shock and I felt quite unnerved by it, as she was only in her early 50s. Whilst meditating she was shown to me behind a mask of smiles – a black, bundle of problems and there was a lot of anguish. I was told that her huge size and her overeating of a lot of meat and cake had contributed to her illness. I had been shown this about someone else I had known who became very ill and died, who ate huge plates of meat and cakes.

I was then shown an entire row of masks of smiling people; behind each one was a mass of black tangles, indicating negative emotions, pain, suffering and lack of forgiveness, wrong foods and lots of stuff locked in. The smiling masks were detached and out front and behind these masks, there were entirely different scenarios going on.

This is because people are keeping in their problems, not healing them, not forgiving, not letting go, not dealing with all this inner turmoil, past events, even past lives. All this stuff is locked into our cells and preventing good health and peace of mind. As we clear, face the problems, forgive and let go, then we purify our cells, our minds, our bodies and our souls.

The way to deal with all this clearing is to meditate regularly and over time, this will gradually bring up these trapped events and feelings and heal them. In addition, one can embark on receiving regular healings, past life therapy sessions, regressions and perhaps embark on some regular workshops.

Events in this life and past lives can cause us great pain and can get locked into our cells and eventually cause us pain and disease. In order to heal and clear pain in the body, we need to look back at when we believe this pain began; look at what may have been going on around that time and then send up a prayer and ask for it to be shifted. We need to let go and forgive any problem connected with the commencement of this pain, we can try to do this ourselves or appoint a healer to do it for us.

By acknowledging a difficult situation or painful occurrence in our life, by letting it go and forgiving those involved, this can then automatically release the negative energies which may be trapped in the body. We can ask the client to send unconditional love and happiness to the area in the body where pain is being experienced; these positive emotions will help to shift the pain. Every cell contains all our experiences and the practice of regular meditation, will automatically and gradually clear our bodies and minds of trapped negative emotions.

One technique to use is to count back slowly through the years of someone's life until the year comes up where there may have been an emotional problem, still locked in. Talking through this with a healer or even dealing with these emotions yourself, possibly by crying, anger and getting out any locked in strong feelings, can release these trapped feelings and release the pain in the body.

This is why regression and past life therapy is very important, we want to be free of locked in emotions so that we have more energy to live our lives the way we are meant to, leading fulfilling lives of creation, happiness and joy.

Whatever circumstances we find ourselves in, there will be reasons and we need to learn many lessons and although this can sound daunting, if we could only try and see what it is we have to learn, the sooner our circumstances will change. For many years, I suffered from not having land and lots of garden, as I am a keen gardener and I found it extremely frustrating. In Somerset, we had two acres of beautiful land; we planted an orchard with many different fruit trees, and had lots of lovely trees, shrubs and flowers and I grew a lot of vegetables. We had chickens, ducks, goats, rabbits, guinea pigs, boxer dog, cats and our horse.

Now with only two small gardens, I gradually realised that I just had to get on with the space I had, and that there is no point in feeling frustrated as this is a negative feeling. This decision brought me peace about the situation. I bought masses of pots and grew all sorts of flowers and vegetables, and had a riot of colour at the front and back of my house. I cannot stop taking cuttings and with no land to plant them, I give them away as presents.

A Curious Event

This took place one evening; I had been attending a spiritual development group run by a friend, and a gentleman who had just joined constantly interrupted talking about scientific theories and challenging every spiritual comment anyone made. I asked him why he was there if he had no spiritual belief, and told him that the way he was speaking was totally inappropriate. He was challenging everything and I felt he should not have been there. I decided not to attend again as I found him very disruptive and irritating. At the end of the session, sensing my discomfort, some dear friends came after me as I left and begged me to come again which was very comforting.

However, as I walked down the road to where my car was parked, I was astonished to see three spirits coming with me, one sat in the front seat of the car and two in the back! They stayed with me all the way home and I thought – what on earth is going on? They came into my home with me and I actually thought they were going to tell me off! Instead, they told me they had come home with me to keep me company and comfort me because they didn't want anybody to upset me; they said they would stay with me all night! I asked who they were and they said 'lesser angels'. Next day, they were gone.

If we can aim to feel happy and grateful, send love to everybody we meet and send love to the world, then everybody and everything around us begins to improve. If we could aim to have more than just positive thoughts and try to have positive happy joyful feelings of love towards everybody, there is no doubt that our life will improve for the better in many ways and the place where we live and surrounding areas will be positively affected.

I have become super aware of my thoughts, words and feelings noticing what is going on around me in terms of vibrations. I am expectant and hopeful and look forward with excitement. I do feel that I am at last beginning to understand vibrations and the power of my thoughts and words, although I am still having to monitor it constantly. Also, we need to build up our self-esteem, and acknowledge our successes however large or small. Gratitude is very important, and an excellent exercise is to think of all the wonderful things that took place in our day when we go to bed at night. We can also write them down. These can be simple things like the sun shining, a pleasant conversation with a friend or neighbour, a lovely walk or a good book we have read. It is essential to be grateful for what we have in our lives, no matter what our circumstances may be, as blessings will then increase.

In the NFSH healing magazine, recently there is a wonderful article about the power of words, and thoughts on water and ice crystals; these experiments have been done by the Japanese scientist, Dr Emoto. Considering we are 80% water, imagine how that will affect us, and how our words and thoughts affect our bodies. When positive words are shown to water, beautiful ice crystals appear. Everything in existence is in a constant state of vibration. Happy people emit happy vibrations. Water circulates around the globe; a river for example is never the same river because its contents are always moving. If we can pray, and send healing and love to the waters of the world, we will be helping to cleanse and purify them.

One night, I had a dream which frightened me a lot. It was connected with some problems I was having from outside sources and I meditated and asked the angels to come close. I called on Jesus, Archangel Chamuel, Archangel Michael, Mother Mary and Kuan Yin. I asked them to come closer and closer and then I saw them right up next to me in a circle holding hands and protecting me; then I saw hundreds upon hundreds of angels in circles ever wider around me until there was about 20 circles deep of angels, all protecting me. I saw someone trying to get through the outside and they could not. It was utterly amazing and I felt safe and deeply grateful.

If this work is new to you and if you have not been used to concentrating on positive thoughts, at first sometimes a lot of negative stuff can come up and fears can deluge you. If you have difficulty or feel negative, a good idea is to concentrate on one particular quality for that day, such as gratitude, and keep it going all day.

Nutrition

As well as our minds, we do need some knowledge about nutrition to also help care for the body, which is the temple of the soul. I find it utterly frustrating how some people do not seem to have the first idea of what or how to eat; it just amazes me. I told my builder who arrived with a stinking cold that he had had for two weeks, to take fresh lemons but I don't believe he bothered. Some people I speak to don't even seem to know what a fresh lemon is. A dear elderly friend of mine in Spain had a heart attack and was very poorly. He had a smallholding where he grew all his vegetables and had lots of fruit trees, and he decided to eat nothing but his own organically grown lemons for two weeks and when he returned to the hospital for a check-up, they could find nothing wrong with his heart. Lemons are very powerful and I was recently sent an article about lemons helping to heal cancer.

A friend of mine was staying with me from Spain and I must have had six fresh lemons in the fridge, and what did she do – she went to the village shop and bought a plastic lemon, which contained preservatives. I simply could not believe it. When I pointed this out, she said it was much easier to squirt lemon juice (which contained preservatives) from the plastic lemon into her tea than cut a slice of fresh lemon and use the juice. I am afraid this is simply beyond my comprehension.

I have met people who never eat fresh vegetables or fruit and who are such physical wrecks that one wonders where their heads are. A neighbour down the road drinks several pints of beer a day, never eats a proper meal, eats no vegetables and fruits, takes endless amounts of pills for depression and wonders why he cannot work and why he shakes from head to toe. I guess we really do have to just let people live and die their own lives in whatever state they choose. We do however need to be aware not to talk endlessly about food and diets as this locks us into body consciousness and we then are not able to fully develop our spirit.

I asked spirit about cancer and I was told that cancer can be caused by anger, fear, chemicals and stagnation. So, we need to rid ourselves of fear and anger, exercise regularly, keep all parts of our bodies moving and eat organically grown foods which are free from chemicals. I have been buying organically grown vegetables for decades, when they were hardly heard of. In Somerset, I used to drive about 20 miles to a farm where a family of big strapping bearded smiling young men in overalls and Wellington boots, would load up my van with piles of vegetables covered in mud. They would explain to me how they grew potatoes bio dynamically according to the moon, which I found fascinating. When I got them home, I would be delighted to find slugs and snails amongst them, proving to me that they were not sprayed with insecticide! I also used to buy half hundredweight sacks of organically grown whole-wheat flour from my local health food shop to bake all my own bread and cakes.

These days, I do not eat wheat or dairy foods. I have found they affect me adversely and are the most common foods to cause allergic reactions in tests I do for my clients. I used to drink Indian tea with milk every half an hour. Now I have one cup in the morning with sheep's milk, which I find more digestible. I gave up coffee for six years at one time when I was teaching yoga as I was so addicted to it and was drinking up to 10 strong cups a day. Whilst abstaining, I used to stop outside a coffee shop in town when passing and longingly inhale the beautiful aromas of coffee beans being ground! I now drink one cup of coffee a day at the most. I drink several mugs of filtered water every day. Again, I have owned a water filter for decades as they filter out a lot of impurities and are simply a must.

I eat fish but I do not eat dead animals, but occasionally eat free range organically fed chicken. When I eat chicken, I pray for that bird and thank it for giving its nourishment to me and my family. I bless all the food I cook and bless all the water I drink. Meat is difficult to digest and contains growth hormones and, chemicals and a great deal of the fear and stress that animals suffer from their treatments and death are taken into their bodies, this then is all taken into our bodies and can sit in the system and cause problems. If you feel you have to eat animals, then try to find naturally reared animals.

One of my nieces refused to ever eat meat again at the age of five, and no matter what my brother and his wife did or said; she flatly refused to listen to them. They were worried about it but she is a tall beautiful girl with wonderful hair and a lovely spirit, and it certainly has done her no harm whatsoever. My own daughter, when she was quite young, gave up meat after seeing a small herd of baby piglets cross the track we were driving on in a remote area in Spain.

Internal Scarring

The main damage done by smoking are the internal scars which take the place of normal cells. Scars are caused by the tars from cigarettes, toxic drugs and nitrites from fertilizers and impurities from foods, air and water.

Scars in arterial walls prevent cholesterol from passing through, thus hastening the onset of heart disease and causing hardening of the arteries. Fats are laid down over the scars and may accumulate quickly until the flow of blood is drastically decreased or completely cut off at certain points. Internal scars are very dangerous. When cells have been damaged or destroyed and the diet is not adequate, scar tissue is formed. Any person who has frequently been ill has dozens of scars inside their body.

Scar tissue cannot function normally or produce necessary hormones. It seems that scarring can be dissolved given time, but the diet has to be fabulous and organic, and vitamin E needs to be taken daily, together with foods very rich in vitamin E, such as whole organic grains and organic cold pressed virgin olive oil. Rosehips, wheat germ and oat bran help to heal the heart. Hydrogenated fats, in many biscuits, cakes and readymade foods, must be completely avoided. *Mooli*, a long white root vegetable that looks like a large carrot but is of the radish family is thought to help heal scarring and also dissolve gallstones. Foods to increase friendly bacteria in the gut are dandelion leaves, garlic, bananas, artichokes, leeks and onions and organic yogurt.

Spiritual Development Groups

As I have mentioned, I have run spiritual development and meditation groups for many years in Somerset, England and in Spain where in one group we had participants of 14 different nationalities. Now living in Devon, a few years ago, I was being encouraged to begin another group and here I share with you some of the experiences we have had. I had very strong feelings on how it should proceed, as I only wanted to contact the very highest spiritual beings of light and love.

A couple of hours before the group arrive, I pray that we will be visited by those who need us the most, and ask for total protection. We begin each meeting by praying for very powerful protection; we ask Archangel Michael to be with us, we can call on him at any time we need protection for ourselves and our homes and journeys. I ask him to surround us all in light. Then we meditate and ask for our guides or any highly evolved spiritual being to come close to us. We ask for any guidance or direction that could help us, or a member of the group. After about half an hour, we then discuss what we see and hear. Not everyone will hear or see but will feel a deep peace of group meditation. Then we close our eyes again and ask for any spirit who needs our help to come forward, or family members and friends who wish to speak to us.

Beautiful beings come through giving us healing and advice: Jesus, Mother Mary, Buddha, angels and Archangels, goddesses including Kuan Yin, the Hindu goddess, and we have seen fairies and other elementals. Each group meeting is different, sometimes family relatives come through for the group members to give messages, love and reassurance. Often an apology is forthcoming for treatment meted out whilst they were alive. We can take the opportunity to send love to our relatives or friends in the spirit world and thank them.

We have all had some very beautiful experiences. Mother Mary came to me and told me she had been with me all my life, I saw myself at school and she told me that she had been with me then and gave me many more wonderful messages and guidance. As we open up to spirit, we may see coloured lights, these are an indication that a spirit, angel or Archangel is with us. There are many different coloured lights indicating different angels. We may also see small white feathers which indicate the presence of angels.

During the group meeting, always strangers arrive, who are stuck and need help to go to the light. I would see queues of people waiting to speak to us, contained by our gatekeeper who is there to protect us from being overwhelmed. The light that is broadcast by a spiritual group will attract people in the spirit world who need help. Also, these meetings are arranged by the spirit world, our guides and helpers, and they know who will come through.

After one session where we had many people who needed help to move to another level, I didn't sleep all night as I was rather concerned about it. I was told that we need to do higher work of helping others when spirit send them to us as we do not need proof of survival because all of us in this group already know that. My development groups are for those who had already been in groups, and not for beginners.

Jesus has come and thanked us as a group for the work we were doing and said there are many groups such as ours and it is a wonderful thing to be doing. If you find this surprising, remember that Jesus said, 'Where two or more of you are gathered in my name, I will be among you'. Many animals visited us thanking us for our prayers and also giving us advice and asking for our help. A dolphin asked us to pray for healing to the seas, the rivers and lakes, that they may be purified and detoxified. An elephant came and thanked me for my prayers, and said that they do help. I now most days pray that every animal that has passed over will rest in peace and I ask that they will be healed in light and love.

We were very blessed to be visited by many ascended masters and enlightened beings. During the very first meeting, we saw Buddha, who appeared crossed legged several feet off the floor; he said he had come for our spiritual enlightenment.

Mother Mary appeared dressed in a beautiful blue cloak and was giving healing to one of the ladies who was having a lot of problems with her daughters. Mother Mary works with families and children. We had a beautiful visitation from King Solomon, who was very tall and dressed regally with a crown, and he gave us advice about manifestation and personal matters.

Over time, we saw St Francis who said we all care deeply for animals and would help us with our prayers. Horus came to help working on our third eye; Nemetona came to protect us. Various Archangels blessed us with their presence and gave us messages. Archangel Chamuel told me he was my house angel and cleared the whole house of all negativity. One lady, who had been to hospital that week for check-ups, had Archangel Haniel next to her with her arms around her, giving her healing.

Other times, we had goddesses with us, Diana, Kuan Yin and Epona. Kuan Yin works with women and told us that we only have to call on her; that she is with all spiritual women. She often comes to me as a bright red light. Maat was also with us and Epona who works with crystals and also horses. She told me to take my large bowl of crystals, soak them in sea salt for an hour and then wash them every two weeks; then carry them from room to room where I am working, use them more, use them with healings, take them to bed, send them love and energy and ask them for this love to be returned to us. I was told that our group and all spiritual groups are extremely important because they are shafts of light which help to heal and elevate the vibrations of the earth, which is vital.

Certainly murderers, rapists and drug addicts, those who are cruel to people and animals do not reach the light on the other side and are in a much darker place until they learn to mend their ways. In one group meeting, a spirit brought forward a soul, a gentleman who informed us that he had murdered many people and was deeply sorry and needed help. He had been in a very dark place for a long time. We are acting as channels and are helped by the spirit world to deal with such cases and as we prayed for him, two spirits came and we saw him being taken away to a healing room. It was obviously time for him to receive the help he so desperately needed. We had a great number of soldiers come to us for help, from many different wars, deeply disillusioned, wounded and lost, and we prayed for them and they were taken to the light, we would see someone come for them and escort them away.

One evening, I suggested we meditate and see what we could pick up regarding the state of the world and all the tragedies taking place with wars and floods... I was told that the earth is undergoing a huge cleansing and clearing, that it is cataclysmic. I asked about certain poor people who were suffering badly in the world, after massive earthquakes and tornados, and was shown all kinds of cruel and unpleasant things from centuries ago which is resulting in some present conditions.

I have been told that earth changes are occurring and light workers are needed to pray for the world and ask for light and love to pour into the earth. We need to try and be peaceful, and not be fearful. We need to keep our thoughts and speech positive and uplifted, especially when discussing what is happening throughout the world. If we are with people who are having fearful discussions about the earth, we need to suggest that they pray for healing to take place in the world and for them to send love and light everywhere it is needed. We need to pray for the earth every day, and ask what we can do to help.

We need to purify our diets, so that we can more easily hear the Divine voice which is trying to guide us. Processed foods block us from hearing guidance clearly. We need simple foods, such as organic brown rice and organic fruits and vegetables that you buy locally or grow yourself. The Earth is alive and loving, and she's taking action to heal herself. Let us ask our angels to watch over our loved ones and us, and help us to hear their guidance in all areas of our lives, including our life purpose.

During one group session, I went into a trance like state and slipped into another life and saw it so clearly it was as though I was really there. I was seated on the ground in a massive Egyptian pyramid, I could feel and see the stone floor vividly, and next to me was a huge stone sarcophagus decorated with very ornate stone carvings. There were people near me who explained that in that life, I had been placed in this tomb for three days in an initiation ceremony. I was then placed in this tomb to experience it again and felt it very acutely. I had already seen this life many years before in meditation but to see and feel it so vividly was startling. When I came around from this state, I felt very strange and it took me a while to adjust to the room and the people with me. I also realised later that this too had been another kind of initiation ceremony. It also became understandable to me why I do not like to be enclosed or be in narrow caves.

Pan

One of my favourite meditations is to see myself slowly rising up through the chakras, the spiritual centres of the body and going up and up to higher realms and reaching Pan, who is a high spiritual Being. He joined us one evening and gave us this message. Each morning, ask spirit for protection to yourself and all your loved ones, animals, homes, vehicles and journeys. There is a lot of turmoil in the world occurring now which can be frightening, stay strong and be positive. Also, see that the earth is wondrous and everyone is a part of God, and try to see the beauty in each person that each one is a beautiful soul, despite appearances sometimes to the contrary. Pray for healing to pour into the world and all the people everywhere. The energies circulating in our group were very powerful and we could feel them healing us.

Then I saw dozens of blackbirds and many other garden birds and they praised and thanked me for caring so deeply for them and protecting them so passionately. That all the birds I have tried to rescue are safe and happy now in the spirit world and send their loving thanks. I saw a snake curl around two of the ladies and myself and was told that it was giving us healing; it was dancing and twirling in front of us. We saw beautiful golden lights surrounding us.

In one of my meditations, reaching Pan I saw hundreds of thousands of animals, and I was told I have prayed for all of them, tigers, all the wild cats, elephants, rhinos and birds and mountain goats (I had forgotten praying for the goats in Spain). I have cried so much about the way animals are treated on this earth and the cruelty they have to endure. I was shown that all are now living in peace with grass, woods, lakes and jungles. Pan appeared and said, "Your prayers are very powerful, every prayer you pray has an effect." I saw it all, and was amazed and felt quite overwhelmed by it all. Most days I send a prayer up for all animals that have passed over that they may be blessed and healed, and live in peace.

I also saw a horse there that I had seen in a hospital. I had been called in to give healing to a gentleman and sat by his bed when I saw a white horse walk through the wall towards me, walk past me and walk through the end wall. I realised that the hospital must have been built on ground where there had been stables or animals. I prayed that this horse be healed and pass into the light so it was quite wonderful to see it again. Curiously, whilst healing a client I saw not only her dogs in the spirit world next to her, but a friend's Great Dane that I had given healing to many years before.

On another occasion, during meditation, I went to Pan where it is very beautiful and peaceful, with sweeping land, lakes, trees, animals and huge birds and I had a very large brown bear with me. I have been praying for all bears, especially the 7000 in China in cages recently announced, and those that are so cruelly treated. I regularly pray for all wild animals that they may be surrounded with love and protection to stop them being hunted.

I have found Pan to be extremely helpful and he has given me some wonderful advice. I was told to pray for self-awareness for two people in my family who were giving me a very hard time. I was a little concerned about this but he said this is a good prayer. He asked me to hand these two people over to him, which I did and he removed them from me to a far distant place. He told me to never let other people influence me or criticise me, that I have important work to do, very profound healings and writing. I asked about my books and he told me to have faith.

One evening, the daughter of one of the ladies in the group who had just returned from Nepal, joined us and brought her Tibetan bowls. These large beautiful bowls are used for healing and are very effective. They are banged gently and give out powerful healing vibrations. As we began this session, I saw Merlin organising various spirits about us and saw black oozing out of us all, as we were being cleared of lower energies in preparation to receive the healing vibrations from the bowls. These are very powerful and I have only experienced them on two occasions, and both times, I was very affected. The first time was in a healing centre and as the gentle sounds were ringing out, I left my body and was floating way above the hall looking down.

We all enjoyed the wonderful effects of this healing and on this occasion, I again went into a trance like state. An amusing side effect of this healing was to my neighbour downstairs. At the time, I was living in an upstairs flat and a good friend of mine was living underneath. I felt it was only polite to warn him before our session that he may hear some Tibetan bowls being used and he wasn't at all bothered to hear this. What was surprising, however, was that he too also went into a trance like state and afterwards, felt much better!

A further note about my friend downstairs, something else around him occurred which was very strange, I was giving him healing one day with a clear blue sky outside and suddenly there was a flash of thunder and lightning and all his electricity blew. Although he felt better afterwards, he wasn't too keen on having more healing! Long after I had forgotten the incident, he was still telling people about it!

Merlin, from the spirit world visited one evening, and I asked how or why he was with us and he bowed and said 'I am at your service' – I said but what do we ask of you? He answered alchemy, healing and manifestation. He told the group to ask him for what they want and to call on him with their desires.

In another session, during the opening prayer, we had a lot of animals in the room looking at us. During the meditation I saw myself covered in frogs and toads, which I love, and a huge lioness lying by my feet. I asked how long the lioness had been with me and she said for many years – to give me strength and she is still with me. We had a whole variety of animals with us, one of the ladies had two birds of prey, an eagle and a hawk; it was all very interesting.

I asked about having animals, birds and fish with us spiritually and what it was all about. I was told that groups of animals are with angels and spirits in the spirit world to add strength, guidance and help. St Francis has thousands of animals with him. We can call on them to help us. I asked about my own animals in the spirit world and was told these animals are always with me due to the love we share.

During one of our sessions, we were told that we need to obtain balance in our lives, but all we do is just rush, rush and rush some more, and nobody just sits. We were advised to just BE sometimes, to meditate much more and be still, not with TV, or radio, or reading a book, but be an empty vessel so that spirit may pour peace, healing and wisdom into us and purify us.

We cannot force spiritual development by simply studying, sitting in circles and going to church, although of course all these things are noble. Our spiritual development involves many aspects of our lives, the way we behave and treat others and ourselves, how we think, how we speak, what we say. Trying hard to be spiritual and to develop can sometimes be counterproductive; it cannot be forced.

We must balance our daily lives and stop the frantic work and rest sometimes. In this regard – by far the best thing to do is to go into a garden or park or open countryside, work with the soil and plants, watch the birds and allow nature spirits to detoxify you, heal you, speak to you and get fresh air and sunlight when you can. Life is not a race; it is a gentle progress. In order for the body to be balanced and whole, our life first has to be balanced with work, rest and fun, social encounters, simple pleasures, some normal pastimes.

At the end of every gathering, we always pray for help to heal the world and ask angels to go to places of war and oppression, to those who are hungry, to the homeless and to the animals. We pray for the forests and jungles to be protected. We can visualise white light pouring into these areas and I regularly pray for love, light and healing to pour into the hearts and minds of all politicians and governments, that they may do the right thing

Prayers are very powerful and join together with everyone else's prayers which give them greater power. They can be very simple; they do not have to be the long and complicated prayers I see suggested sometimes. I pray fervently every day for protection to the elephants, wild cats, rhinos, bears and other animals so cruelly hunted, and ask that those who are trying to help be empowered and supported. One of the mediums was picking up mermaid energy with me and that is why I have always felt very passionate about whales and dolphins and thoroughly support Greenpeace with their work.

I choose to believe that we most certainly can do something about the world, and prayers, as I have been told and as I have witnessed, are extremely powerful. I recall a time when I intensely prayed for an area in India that was desperately short of water and I read a few weeks later that an underground river had been discovered in the area, which was able to supply that whole region with good fresh water. I like to think that my prayers may have helped.

A neighbour who had passed into the spirit world came through to our group one evening; he was brought by an angel or guide. He was a lovely man and I had helped him when he was dying, he had asked for me to call on him and I gave him regular healing which greatly comforted him and made him feel much more peaceful. I also taught him to meditate and to pray, and call on angels and spirit help. He came through to thank me for all I did for him. His wife had given me a big box of garden bulbs afterwards, and I thanked him for those.

He gave me some more personal messages and then said that he was so glad that he had served in our local neighbourhood watch, which links to the police and social services, as service is so beneficial; it elevates you to a different level here in the spirit world. He said he was very grateful for the help he had received as it made him feel a lot better. He said how extremely beneficial it is to be aware of our neighbours and help them when we can. Healing, even though the person may have a terminal illness, is normally extremely helpful, calming and supportive and can alleviate a person's fears about passing over.

Outdoor Spirits

During one of our sessions, I was told that outside the fairies and nature spirits need love and gratitude; that we just take them all for granted, and we need to send them love and acknowledge their presence and they in turn will then send us healing and clean us up, and clean our aura if we take the time to sit there and ask. They need more respect and acknowledgement. I was given a glimpse of how it would be if we could see them all, the whole garden was alive with little creatures everywhere.

As we develop, our clairvoyant sight opens more and more and during a recent healing, I was astonished to 'see' a gnome for the first time stood by the side of my client. He stood about three feet away just looking at us. As I knew nothing about gnomes, I had no idea why he was with me and as he didn't speak, I felt I had to do some research afterwards.

Gnomes, fairies and all other nature spirits have been seen for thousands of years and in ancient times, it was perfectly normal to see them. So many people now have closed minds with regard to these matters and through ignorance; ridicule is common.

It appears that the first person who made serious documentation on gnomes and other elementals was Paracelsus, born in 1493, a Swiss scholar, physician, occultist, alchemist and astrologer, who studied medicine at Basel University, later moving to Vienna. He gained his doctorate degree from the University of Ferrara, in northern Italy. A medieval scholar, he wandered as an itinerant physician through many countries of Europe, working as a practising astrologer, as were most if not all of the university trained physicians working in Europe at this time. Astrology was a very important part of Paracelsus' medicine, using talismans for curing disease. He also pioneered the use of chemicals and minerals in medicine. He was a healer, an original thinker and learned the philosophy of spiritual substance.

He revised old manuscripts and wrote new ones, and finally gained fame with his published work in 1536, *The Great Surgery Book*. This man was unique in pioneering the harmony of man's health, with theories about imbalances in the body. He wrote many other major works, including theories in psychotherapy and books about the elementals.

It is therefore, fascinating that this highly skilled and learned man should see these nature spirits. Furthermore, there are writings about the dialogues between Plato and Socrates, around 300 BC that indicate an understanding about elementals. Rudolf Steiner, an Austrian philosopher who founded a spiritual movement and created educational institutions, has lectured extensively on gnomes and especially their supportive role in the development of plant life and biodynamic agriculture and had a great deal to say about the spirit worlds and nature spirits, angels and Archangels. He asserted that humanity would be unable to reconnect with the spiritual world if it cannot develop a new relationship to the elementals. He went on to say that the nature spirits want to be of great assistance to us acting as emissaries of higher divine spiritual beings. We do of course first need to acknowledge their presence and develop a relationship with them.

Although supposedly mythical, gnomes and other elementals have been seen for thousands of years and all over European lands, there are tales of sightings and legends. They live in natural areas close to the earth and care for wildlife, tending to wild animals that are sick. They don't like the sun and some sources claim that they spend hours during daylight as toads. One thing for certain is that they are friendly and require respect and acknowledgement. In the works of Paracelsus, he claims gnomes are the earth spirits, undines relate to the water, sylphs to the air and salamanders are fire elementals. Tree and forest sprites include sylvestres, satyrs, pans, dryads, hamadryads, durdalis, elves and brownies.

Every plant has its own nature spirit and during the development circles, we have been told to respect these spirits, acknowledge them and take more care with our plants, request permission before cutting them, and generally develop a relationship with these creatures, who in turn can help us considerably. They have healing abilities and if we meditate outside, we can tune in to these creatures and receive much guidance. There are thousands of creatures everywhere with all the plants, bushes and trees and as we train and open our third eye, we will begin to see them. My gnome spoke to me at a later date and said that this will be a gradual process, due to the fact that we would not otherwise be able to cope with it, although we have a great many spirits around us all the time.

I have recently been listening to a CD by R Ogilvie Crombie, a very well-spoken and logical scientist, who lectured and wrote about his experiences seeing fairies and gnomes, elves and nature spirits and having talks with Pan. He has lectured at Findhorn in Scotland, and his experiences with the nature kingdom have been included in a book written at Findhorn. He, evidently at the age of four, wished to see fairies and at the age of 67 or 68, he saw them! He was born in 1899 and he died in 1975 aged 76. It seems we have to be prepared, bodily, emotionally and spiritually before we can see them. That we have to have proper motives and then they come to us; that they are much more powerful than we can possibly imagine.

There have been hundreds of sightings of gnomes in Argentina recently in a village there, and although some have been photographed, it is not known whether these are for real or not. In Iceland, gnomes are so respected that roads are said to be rerouted around areas thought to be inhabited by them.

A while ago, the fairies told me they want me to be totally free of fears. Ganesh came and I saw my affairs sewn up like a cushion, all stitched up around the edges, for protection. Ganesh is the Hindu elephant god who can clear obstacles if we ask him. I asked how one could overcome personal karma. I was told that killing someone cannot be overcome by normal means but for the rest – forgiveness is the first key and after that, it is kindness.

One member of our group heard and saw a nature spirit called Alanthe and I meditated to find out who she is. I waited a while and then I heard a voice saying rather crossly 'I am a very powerful fairy' – I asked are you from ancient Greece, she said it doesn't matter where she is from although she did emanate from there around 5000 years ago, she is with us now, that is what is important. I said but we don't know anything about you – she said you will hear from many more people who you have never heard about before. I asked why she seemed a bit cross – she said you don't realise how much we can help you or how powerful we are – you think that we are lesser beings but we are not, we have great power and we need to be recognised and appreciated. She said she gathers forces to help us in our group meetings.

I respectively asked what, in fact, she and other elementals are doing for us. She said they are clearing us of negativity and lower energies which we are constantly picking up every day, and unless we clear ourselves every night and protect ourselves every morning and each time we go out and are around other people, negative thoughts and words attach themselves to us. When we listen to the news – which they constantly tell us not to do – when we read the newspapers, or when we entertain negative thoughts, fears and worries, this all affects our auras. She said that they are working on us to clear these negative vibrations from us. She said that she and the fairy kingdom could help us so much more if we would only ask. They are waiting to be asked. Sitting outside amongst flowers and near trees is the best place to commune with nature spirits.

I attend my local spiritualist church and at the end of the service, a group of healers give healing to those who need it. As I am a member of the National Federation of Spiritual Healers, which is a different organisation, I do not give healings there. I do, however, often sit at the back of the room and pray for white light and healing for everyone. On these occasions, I often see a variety of spirits and on one occasion, I could vaguely see my gnome, so I asked if I could see him more clearly. He had a large nose, a beard, hairy face and red and green garments.

I asked him if he was serious, unhappy or surly as he wasn't smiling, but he said, "No, not at all." I saw him smile later. He said he has been with me for a long time, and I am surrounded by a great many spirits, I asked why I don't see them all the time. He reminded me that I had been really astonished the first time I had seen him; he said imagine how you would feel to see lots about you all the time. He said you will see spirits one at a time, gradually, so that you can cope with them.

He also informed me that when I see gold and purple swirling lights, these would be nature spirits. These coloured lights are surreal and utterly beautiful. On one occasion, I saw a flying creature in the middle of these swirling coloured lights. One evening, during our group meeting, we saw dolphins leaping about and everybody in the group saw them. At the third eye, I saw a huge eye – Horus – he said he is permanently with me.

Feeling Overwhelmed

At a time when someone was putting me under a lot of pressure, and I was very busy writing and involved with my family; I was told to see myself in the centre of a circle with a fence around me, and to move the fence further and further away from myself and keep this person and anybody else putting me under pressure on the other side. I was told very firmly, "We are empowering you – to be strong and stand firm, do your writing, and don't let anyone upset you, pester you or pressure you, just say no." This is a good exercise for anyone who feels beleaguered into unwanted activities or relationships.

One day I was feeling intensely pressured by work, writing, so many people to deal with, phone calls and emails, and I was suddenly aware of a visitation from Maharishi Mahesh Yogi, the founder of Transcendental Meditation, who passed into the spirit world a few years ago. He told me that pressures are self-inflicted. He told me to ignore phones, ignore emails, – "There you are," he said, "you have joy, you are free!" Then I heard him laughing, much bubbling laughter, much joy. This was something he did a great deal of – laughing. It had a major effect on me and I was overcome with astonishment and wonderment that he was with me, giving me advice. It helped me enormously. I then saw myself inwardly putting everything and everybody into a basket and tipping it all away, everything – people, books, worries, fears, pressures, everything.

He then gave me some personal advice about my relationships and told me that my books will be published, to have no doubt, and to hand it all over to God. I asked how it was that he was speaking to me when there are at least three and a half million people practising transcendental meditation and he said you have meditated a long time and you have a huge light around you.

Then some while later, I was meditating again, feeling very depressed after yet another local funeral of a neighbour – the third one. I also felt bogged down with concerns about one of my neighbours who was constantly waylaying me and gossiping and I was also fretting a bit about money. Once again, Maharishi came and spoke to me and he said put all this behind you. He said do not concern yourself with these funerals as you did not know these people very well, you have your own relationships, projects, home and life and to this lady who was waylaying me, you say hello and back away. And, you have enough money for your needs, be patient. This and the last communication, helped me so much, it was staggering.

Another time I had a very amusing experience when again I was feeling under pressure. I was meditating and went to Pan in the spirit world and I told him my printer isn't working, am under pressure with so much to do and I saw about three dozen gnomes fall on their backs in hysterics, laughing, they said we don't have those problems. I felt a bit hurt and said but these problems are important to me – I need my printer, still they continued to laugh, until I began to feel bubbles of joy and laughter welling up in me. Pan said you will sort all these problems out, they are nothing in the grand scheme of things, lighten up, the laughter was to help you lighten up – it did help me hugely and I continued to laugh for a couple of hours!

On one occasion, I was feeling uneasy and unhappy and so I went into the garden and began meditating, and asked the nature spirits to help me. I said there are so many interruptions, so many problems to deal with, and I was finding it very difficult to get on and write this book. I was having problems with my teeth, there were difficult neighbours next to a property I rent out, our boiler wasn't working and the house was freezing, we had a leak in the roof and I asked how on earth was I supposed to deal with so many problems and find time to continue writing.

The answer was quite amazing. I was told – What if you believed and knew, that no matter what obstacles, what problems, what distractions life throws at you, you will still achieve your goals, you will get published, what if you knew that and had faith, how would you feel then? Don't think the obstacles are there to stop you, just see them as life and know that you will still achieve your goals at the right time and in the right way. Hearing this seemed to lift the frustration off me and give me fresh hope and energy

A good affirmation is 'let go and let God'. I found this really helpful to practise as I seemed to be stuck with my writing for a while, and I was getting worried and stressed about it. I decided to really let go, hand it over to God and relax instead of feeling uptight. I was practising this for a few days and saying I am happy and successful anyway. Suddenly, I felt able to write again. I was practising letting things go, letting everything go, accepting how things are. We need to try not to resist anything. We need to learn to let go, then possibilities open up and we act on them, we naturally do things and become happier. I was saying I am already perfect now, I am enough now. I was allowing and adapting to the way things are, instead of struggling. When we let go, and especially when we let go and let God, things seem to work out easily and effortlessly. We can also send love to any problem we have and this helps to shift it. Just feel love and healing pouring into whatever is troubling us.

I was also told that spirit want us to love ourselves so much more, appreciate ourselves and congratulate ourselves for all of our achievements, big and small. I was told to go outdoors more often and listen to nature spirits. Also, we need to realise that we are unlimited and can achieve anything and everything we desire. These beliefs change our vibrations and we then attract more good into our life, the higher and better we believe ourselves to be, the more we will receive.

The prouder we are of ourselves and the more powerful we know ourselves to be, the better our lives will be with stronger auras and vibrations. Never see yourself as weak, tired, unaccomplished, neurotic, unorganised or chaotic. See yourself as strong, capable, clever, organised, powerful, beautiful, skilful and adaptable. The nature spirits told me that they were so relieved to impart this knowledge.

They then told me how much they appreciated my love of nature, birds, animals and my prayers for the world and the nature kingdom. They told me I am deeply loved and that it is a great joy to them that I can feel and hear them. They then advised me to send love to anybody I do not like or who is causing me problems.

I was also told that we all need to have and learn patience. Patience with life, patience with our situation, our relatives, our dreams, everything. Instead of struggling against situations, we need to accept them, look at them, see how best we can improve them, see the opportunity there may be, take responsibility, but accept and find peace within no matter what is occurring. This is a very profound spiritual teaching which could help us enormously once we grasp it.

The Passing of Children

In one of our group sessions, one of the women was told that when children pass, they go into the nature kingdom. I tuned in and asked about this and was told the following.

Every soul is individual and there are no set rules about where souls go or how they pass. Each case depends on their spiritual state at the time; how they have lived their life, what their karma is and the reasons for being born and then leaving, and so on. Some very small children feel more comfortable when they pass over to be with the nature kingdom, with animals, flowers and other creatures. They may spend some time in this realm and then move to another realm when they are ready.

Also, when a child dies, it is more appropriate to come back as this child for the benefit of grieving relatives, as they are then recognisable, rather than appearing as a grown up version. I asked if children do grow up in the spirit world and was told that they do, as and when it is appropriate, that once again, there are no rules; it depends on their progress and their needs. Some grow in different ways; it all depends on their lives and reasons for being born and leaving.

I myself had a miscarriage before my first son was born, and one day during meditation, I suddenly saw a young woman about 20 years old and knew who she was. At the time, it was a shock and I was very upset, as I had never seen her before and had not known what sex my baby would have been, and wasn't even sure if a soul could have entered so early a pregnancy, as I had only been a few weeks pregnant.

Speaking in Tongues

I was quite disturbed about this friend of ours who is frequently lapsing into 'speaking in tongues' and as it is mentioned in Corinthians 1 verse 12 as being one of the spiritual gifts we can be given, I was wondering what it is all about. I couldn't see much point in it. I, fortunately, the next day (amazingly well organised by spirit!) met a friend who is involved in running the spiritualist church and we had a good chat about it and she agreed with me and told me to trust my gut instinct, that she also could see no point in lapsing into tongues which nobody can understand. She also agreed with me that it is uncontrolled and as this friend of ours was seriously ill last year, we agreed it is not a good idea.

It occurs to me – *who can these spirits be who speak in various languages?* – They can't be from the very highest realms, or else they would surely speak in a language which we can understand. I personally think it is fine to channel philosophy but again only if this comes from a very high spiritual source. I think channelling philosophy needs to be listened to carefully and if it sounds of a very high quality, makes perfect sense, then fine. Trivial stuff coming through makes me question the point of that too, and also makes me wonder at what level is the spirit operating. I have personally found that some of the channelled stuff I have heard can be confusing. I am not judging, just simply being acutely aware of everything said and not just accepting and assuming that it is coming from a high level, simply because somebody has gone into trance.

Even the Bible says the following:

Corinthians. 14. 22: Tongues then are a sign, not for believers but unbelievers; prophecy, however, is for believers, not for unbelievers.

Corinthians. 1. 14. 27–28: If there is no interpreter, the speaker should keep quiet.

I recall a born again Christian neighbour who attended a church and someone there would go into a trance and she and everyone at the church was highly impressed saying this was proof of God and his power. Therefore, I think the above is correct, that trance can help prove to people who need it, that there is a higher power operating.

I remember in a large spiritual development group of 36 people in Fuengirola, Spain, a lady who was sat next to me suddenly went into a trance and was speaking in a language that I certainly did not understand. However, we had a Paraguayan in our midst and he was able to confirm that it was an ancient native language which he recognised.

Gurus and Spiritual Leaders

Here I would like to say some words of caution about gurus and spiritual leaders. From experience, I believe we really must stay strong and follow our own path. We can most definitely be guided and learn to meditate, but we need to stand back and listen and not to hang on to every word that we are told. There have been quite a number of gurus who have turned out to be rogues and false.

In the beginning on a spiritual path, people are searching searching, searching, and it is fine to visit ashrams, gurus and spiritual centres, but, eventually, we need to search inside ourselves, if we learn to listen to our inner voice, we will understand so much more. Spiritual development groups can be very powerful if the participants are sincere and positive, and group energy can open us up more quickly, but, again, care needs to be taken.

For instance, I had several people in one of my yoga classes who were always trying to turn me away from the transcendental meditation I was practising and join their meditation group, and I always told them I was perfectly happy and had no desire to join them. They had a guru who seemed to be telling them how to live down to the last detail. They even named their children from what this guru said, and he told them what to eat. When this so-called guru, who appeared to have about 100 Rolls-Royces, then disappeared to India from South Africa, as I understand it, with millions of pounds of devotees' monies, they were devastated and totally disillusioned.

One of the women, who had been in my yoga class for some time, was so shocked, she felt unable to trust anyone and was highly suspicious of me and my teachings and was unsure whether to continue with her yoga practice. Each week, she would stay behind after the class and talk to me for some time, and I did manage to persuade her that practising yoga was perfectly safe and I was totally trustworthy.

Even though I learned transcendental meditation, I didn't get carried away with hanging on to Maharishi's every word; I got on with my meditation daily and regularly and developed my own strength and understanding. Someone once asked Maharishi what they should eat, and his answer was – Eat what your mother told you! I recall one of the meditation teachers informing me that Maharishi would not have approved of what I was wearing on that particular day! Needless to say, I wear what I like and eat what I think fit; I also name my children as I please. We really must maintain our own strength and think carefully about what we are told and not follow others blindly.

There is yet another guru who was worshipped like a god, and although he did much for charity before he died, he was in the end exposed as a fraud, with very serious allegations made against him. Millions of people worshipped this man and I know someone who had an altar dedicated to him and called him God. Unfortunately, for people who devote their whole lives to a guru of this nature, they can then not face the brutal facts of their guru's downfall, as it would negate their whole life and their whole belief systems.

Develop yourself, listen by all means to everyone, read everything you want but be careful, take on board only that which you feel to be true, dedicated regular meditation will bring about all you desire spiritually, but you need patience. Talk to God, Jesus, Mother Mary, Buddha, Mohammed, Hindu goddesses, angels, Archangels or whichever spiritual deity you believe in, ask for guidance and help on your spiritual path, but remember that God is within us and within everything and everyone. Realise you are powerful yourself and develop your own understanding, rather than hanging on to other people's words and beliefs. Depending on our development and spiritual progress, we all have a slightly different understanding of spirituality, this doesn't mean we are right and someone else is wrong or vice versa. It is very important to develop our own understanding. Praying and asking for help, having faith and patience can bring about guidance and understanding.

Loving Beings

As I have said, in the spiritual development groups in my home, we always asked for beings from the highest source of love and light to join in. Many wonderful beings came. We saw Isis, this ancient goddess is the mother of Horus, the one-eyed falcon-headed pharaoh; she married Osiris, and Seth, his brother, killed him. Isis brought him back to life, and they conceived Horus. Then Seth killed him again and chopped him into pieces so that he could not be revived. Horus then went after Seth and lost an eye. Horus helps us with clairvoyance and we often see him.

Lakshmi, a beautiful Hindu goddess, came and showered us with silver dust from a wand, she said she was showering us with prosperity. Then the Eastern goddess, Kuan Yin, was above us, cross-legged in the air, and above her was the spirit of love and light, a huge powerful force pouring down white light on and around us, sending us colours, blue, green, yellow, orange and silver into our chakras and auras. Mother Mary came to us on many occasions. One time, I saw her open up the top of my head and put in a white feather.

I was told that we had a permanent pyramid around us from the power of Atlantis; this was giving us very gentle healing and protection. I have been told to ask for this powerful positivity-loving Atlantean energy to be used to heal the world. There were many mixed energies in the world of Atlantis, some positive and some negative.

I saw two members of our group with dark areas in their auras and was told they had emotional blocks which needed clearing. When they are meditating, they need to tune into this, and crying will help to relieve it, but neither of them could cry. Also, we picked up that one of the group members had had an awful experience as a child with a man and the experience and pain of it was still locked inside her. She was told to cut the ties that bind with an axe, and we helped her to do that.

Ties need to be cut to people, especially to those who may be giving us a hard time or to people we feel angry with or who have impacted our life in a negative way. You can do this during meditation. Sit quietly and breathe deeply for a minute or two and then gently, with eyes closed, try to imagine that person sat opposite you. Look to see if you are joined in any way, this can be with cord, metal or any number of attachments, to various points of the body. You can tell how powerfully they are tied to you, by the ties that you see.

You can then ask for help and see these cords being cut in half, pulled out and burnt. This frees both people. Depending on the ties, you can imagine using various methods of getting rid of them, scissors, a sword and, in strong metal ties, a saw. See the root into yourself being pulled out gently and see the root in the other person also being pulled out. Pile these ties on to a bonfire and burn them.

We did work on this in our group, one lady had very strong ties still to her ex-husband and another person, and the ties went through her and through the other two people, tying them all into a circle. Another had a very strong tie to a close relative who had passed over. These ties take away our strength.

One evening, I saw the father of one of the group member standing in front of her dressed in black from head to toe. He had been down, depressed and lonely during his lifetime and this had made him very difficult to live with. He asked for her forgiveness and said he hadn't really understood life. He then knelt in front of her, held her hands and said he desperately needed her love. He was stuck and had not gone into the light. She said she forgave him and sent him love.

He said that we all need to be happy. That there is no point in worrying, being anxious, unhappy, lonely or depressed, we must find a way to be happy, it is a matter of learning how. We need to find things that make us happy, such as fondling animals, tending a garden, enjoying flowers, taking a walk, whatever makes us happy. He said life goes by so quickly it is pointless to be anything other than happy. When he had finished speaking, I then asked for a shaft of light to come down over him and help him to move on. I then saw him disappear up and into this tube of light.

I was also told earlier that several spirits we would not know would come to us later. Most of us saw various people with names none of us knew. We then saw a learning group, people in a huge circle around us, we were being used as a lesson in the spirit world, all the beautiful colours and light around us had attracted them. One of the women felt this was a kind of University. These were spirits who were practising coming through to a group, curious to see the lights.

One time, a tall man came and introduced himself as St Germain, "I am with you permanently, guiding and uplifting you." He gave me some personal messages and then told me about clearing the space in the room where I write, in order to raise the vibrations, and to do this as soon as possible and stick at it. This was good advice as there were lots of papers that needed filing and sorting, piles of my manuscripts and I was struggling to deal with it all. His encouragement helped me to tackle it all. I thanked him so much and have talked to him a lot since then. It seems that in previous incarnations, he was born as Joseph, the father of Jesus, Shakespeare, Christopher Columbus, Francis Bacon, Merlin and many more extraordinary people. He is at a very high level of light and love.

On the day of the memorial service of Princess Diana, to mark 10 years since she died, I felt her near me when I was meditating. I had been feeling cross about a certain member of the Royal family who seemed to be taking a lot of liberties. She said the following, "We choose to be born in certain situations so why judge anyone, you may not agree with the principle of royalty but each person is acting a part, try not to judge them. You have been and are much happier than I was; you still have your children and their love and presence. You've had a much better life than me. If for instance, as you think this person takes liberties, it is his soul that pays. Concentrate on your own soul and learn quickly not to judge."

This lovely lady came through at a later date to our spiritual development circle and several participants saw her. She told us she was attracted to the light, which circles generate. She said she misses her two sons very much and is very proud of them.

She said she would love us to give them that message but knew it was impossible as we would not be able to get near them.

Many years ago when my clairvoyance was beginning to open up, I used to ask people if they had a lady in spirit called Alice, they would say no, and I would say well she is standing here. This continued for about two years and I found it very strange. Then one day, it dawned on me that she was with me! I felt very embarrassed and apologised to her, the poor woman had been trying to make contact with me and I had not realised. She was my great aunt Alice, I remember meeting her in Yorkshire when I was a child, she was a large lady and a wonderful artist, I have one of her oil paintings on my wall, it is beautiful. Since then she has visited me many times and is always urging me to pick up my paintbrushes and paint. I am a potter and I have done some painting and would like to do some more when I have time!

When our clairvoyant sight begins to open up, it can be very bewildering. I remember the first time I saw a spirit when I was in a development circle in the early days, he was a Zulu, he looked quite terrifying and he told me he was with me and protecting me. Immediately afterwards, I then saw a group of native Indians who were in a circle and they all jumped up and down gleefully and were dancing. I was completely mystified by this and wondered what on earth was going on. Over the following few days I realised that the native Indians had been overjoyed that I had at last begun to 'see', and were rejoicing.

I know that many things I am writing about may be very strange to the reader, but whilst writing this book, I have been told by spirit not to hold back and to say what I wish and not be afraid. I was told to write about everything and not fear what others think as this is very important. During a group meditation, a medium saw my lioness next to me and told me that this related to me having a powerful female voice and I needed to speak out!

Benefits of Spiritual Development

I was thinking about the Kundalini energy which had been unleashed in me many years ago, and what effect it had been having. I meditated about it and was given a very full answer. After many years of Kundalini energy, meditation and spiritual development, there will be some very positive changes.

The average Mrs Jones, who is not involved with spiritual development, worries about everything. She will run to the doctor for every small thing, she thinks the doctor knows best and slavishly follows his advice without ever thinking for herself. Mrs Jones is afraid of dying. She moans about everything. She never has enough money. Mrs Jones blames everybody else for the problems in her life. She has no idea about nutrition and her body, exercise and energies. Mrs Jones isn't sure about God even though she may go to church. She talks about old age, illnesses, poverty, and the terrible state of the world. She does nothing to help the world, she doesn't pray, and just takes on board all the bad news. She expects to go into a nursing home.

The average Mrs Jones has no peace of mind, no faith, no spiritual understanding, knows nothing about the spirit world, angels, or the nature kingdom even though she may go to church. The average Mrs Jones is very critical and judgmental. She wouldn't believe in healers, other worlds, miracles, self-healing, fasting or mediums. She wouldn't understand seeing beautiful colours in meditation or glimpses of other worlds. The average Mrs Jones is stuck in a rut mentally with fixed ideas and beliefs.

So to sum up, spiritual development, meditation and Kundalini awakening bring about knowledge, peace of mind, acceptance, gentleness, power, energy, love, kindness, gratefulness and higher qualities of the soul. Spiritual energies clear us, cleanse us, bring out hidden pain and unforgiveness, and help us to develop and grow, believe in ourselves and bring about peace of mind, lightness of spirit, fun and happiness. Life should be in three parts, one part spiritual activities, one part earning one's living and practical things and one part joyful celebrations with family and friends with, of course, spiritual values running throughout. We need to enjoy the earth and its gifts, and have fun and laughter.